MAKE & DO

BECI ORPIN

25 amazing projects
to beautify your life

hardie grant books
MELBOURNE · LONDON

CONTENTS

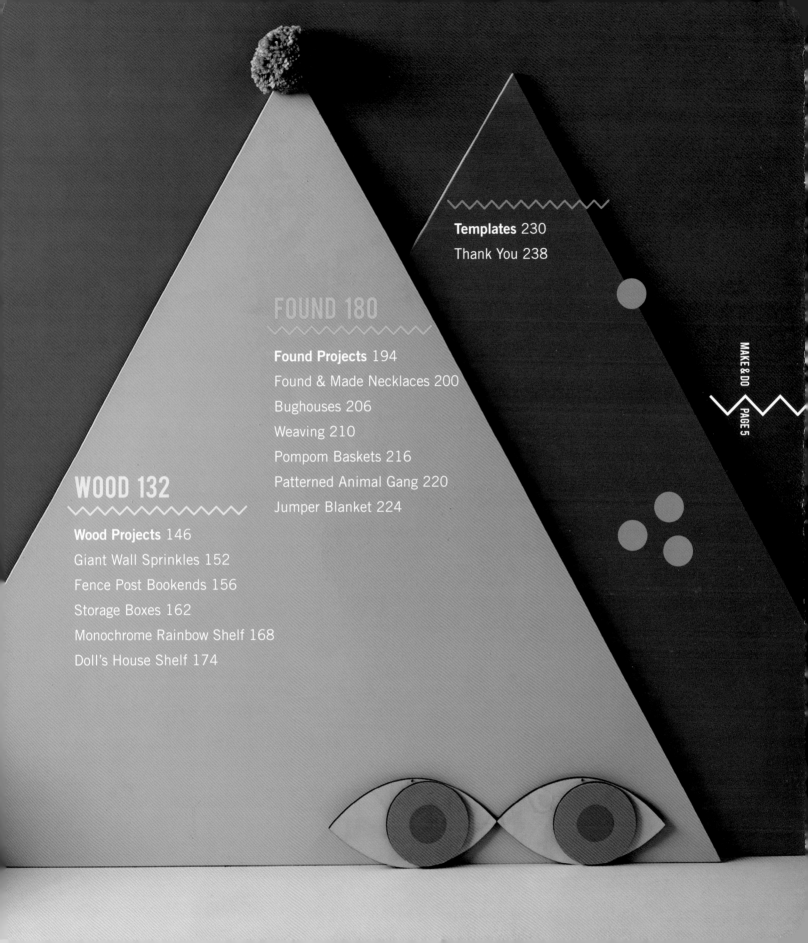

Thank you to all the people who have supported me, bought my books and artwork, come to my workshops or just said nice things.

DEDICATION

INTRODUCTION

OH MY GOSH! Book number three – what a treat! I'm pinching myself that I am up to my third book.

This book is based around one of my favourite subjects – the spaces where we make and do creative things. For me that's usually in my studio, but sometimes at my dining room table, on the couch in front of the TV, or even with a bunch of pencils and paper on the floor (Ari style).

It's also quite apt that I was able to make a book about creative spaces and studios, because this year there was a big change in regards to where I do all my work. I moved from my much-loved home studio into a new space – a perfect ten-minute bike ride away – which I share with my partner, Raph, and his food businesses. We had the absolute luxury of having it designed and built by our friend and architect Julian Patterson. Working in this new space is a dream come true and makes me feel very grown up indeed.

It does have its downfalls, though. After six years of working in my home studio, I had become accustomed to certain things. The natural light there was perfect, I had my cats to keep me company, and when I wanted to make something with the boys all my art supplies were on hand. With my new studio I now no longer have these things. Other logistics such as working across two computers and family responsibilities (basically who is doing the school pick-up) all need to be sorted out as well.

While I was making this book, I was lucky enough to visit and photograph many of my friends' studios and creative spaces. I was surprised how different they all were. Some people had warehouses with employees, others worked out of their bedrooms, some studios had walls completely covered in images and were jam-packed with towers of books, while other spaces were beautifully minimal. Each studio was incredibly individual and had its own personality, yet no matter what kind of studio it was, the work that came out of it was amazing.

After these visits and my own studio move, I came to a realisation. I love my new fancy studio but it's not a necessity in order to make nice things. Although it may have made my work more professional (no more surprise kids' undies on chairs or cats jumping onto allergic clients during meetings), it hasn't necessarily made my work better. I think that as long as you have the materials you need and you surround yourself with things that inspire you, you can turn just about anywhere into a creative space – whether it's a temporary space, such as a coffee table, or a more permanent one, such as the corner of your bedroom.

Each of the chapters in this book is based around the materials I love to use in my studio: textiles, paper, wood and found (or recycled) objects. I love each of these materials for its own unique reasons, so it was such a joy to have the chance to develop new and creative ways of using them. I'm glad I can share these projects with you and I hope you enjoy them as much as I do.

TEXTILES

I studied Textile Design at uni, so textiles are an obvious choice of medium for me. To be honest, I didn't really know what it would entail – it just seemed like a good course where I would be able to draw. I applied and, to my surprise, I got in. Once I started and began to learn all the ins and outs of screen printing, weaving and knitting, my love for all things textile was solidified. As with many things in my life, when a love blooms, a collection soon follows.

My textile collection is in my studio and is surprisingly well organised into boxed categories, such as 'retro children's prints', 'Asian silks' and 'embroideries and cross-stitches'. In truth, I forget about them most of the time, but once every six months or so I pull them out and pore over them.

Unlike some of my other collections, I don't think I could ever part with my textiles. Many of them are handmade, and while some don't necessarily have a monetary value, I appreciate how much thought and effort has gone into making them – it's the history of these pieces that holds the most value to me.

I am also a sucker for a fabric store, and try not to visit them too often because I never walk out empty handed. Don't even get me started on trims and haberdashery; I drool at the mere thought of walking down those aisles! My fabric and trim purchases are sorted into different drawers, to use in future projects. Some of the projects in this book are made from the spoils of those drawers, so things do get put to good use (eventually).

We visited and photographed lots of studios and while all of them were beautiful and inspirational, it was the more textile-based studios that were my idea of heaven. Textiles are such a wonderfully tactile medium. Even now, when I see a pile of fabric or yarn, the child in me still wants to make a cubbyhouse fort out of stacks of fabric and live cosily in there for a few days, possibly sewing or latch hooking the floors and walls while I'm there.

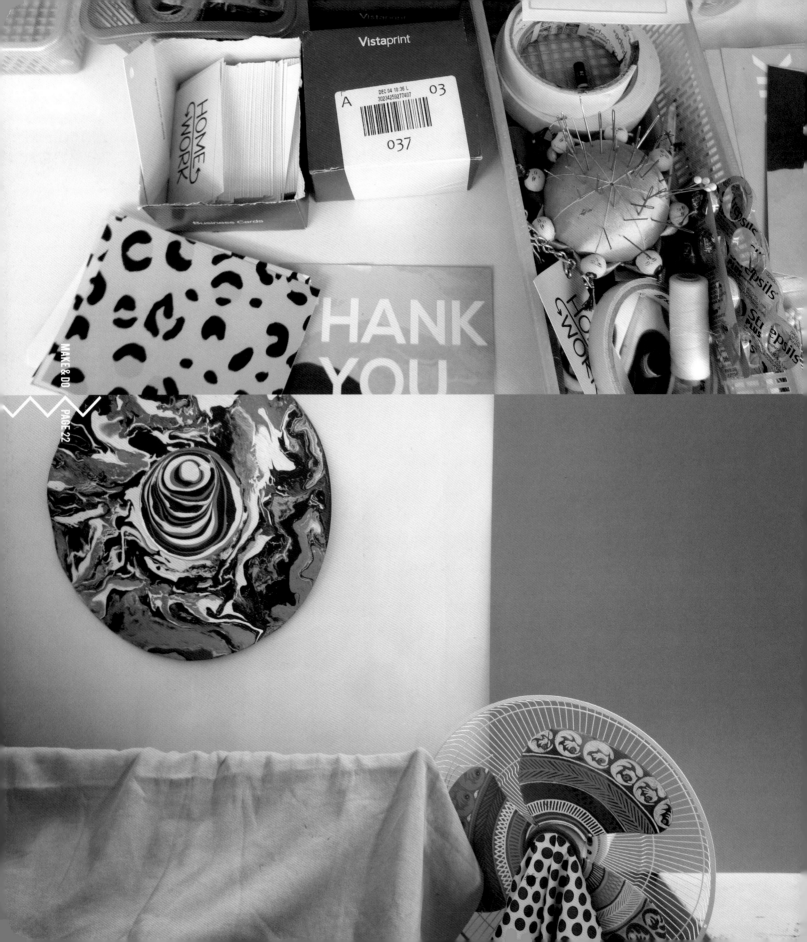

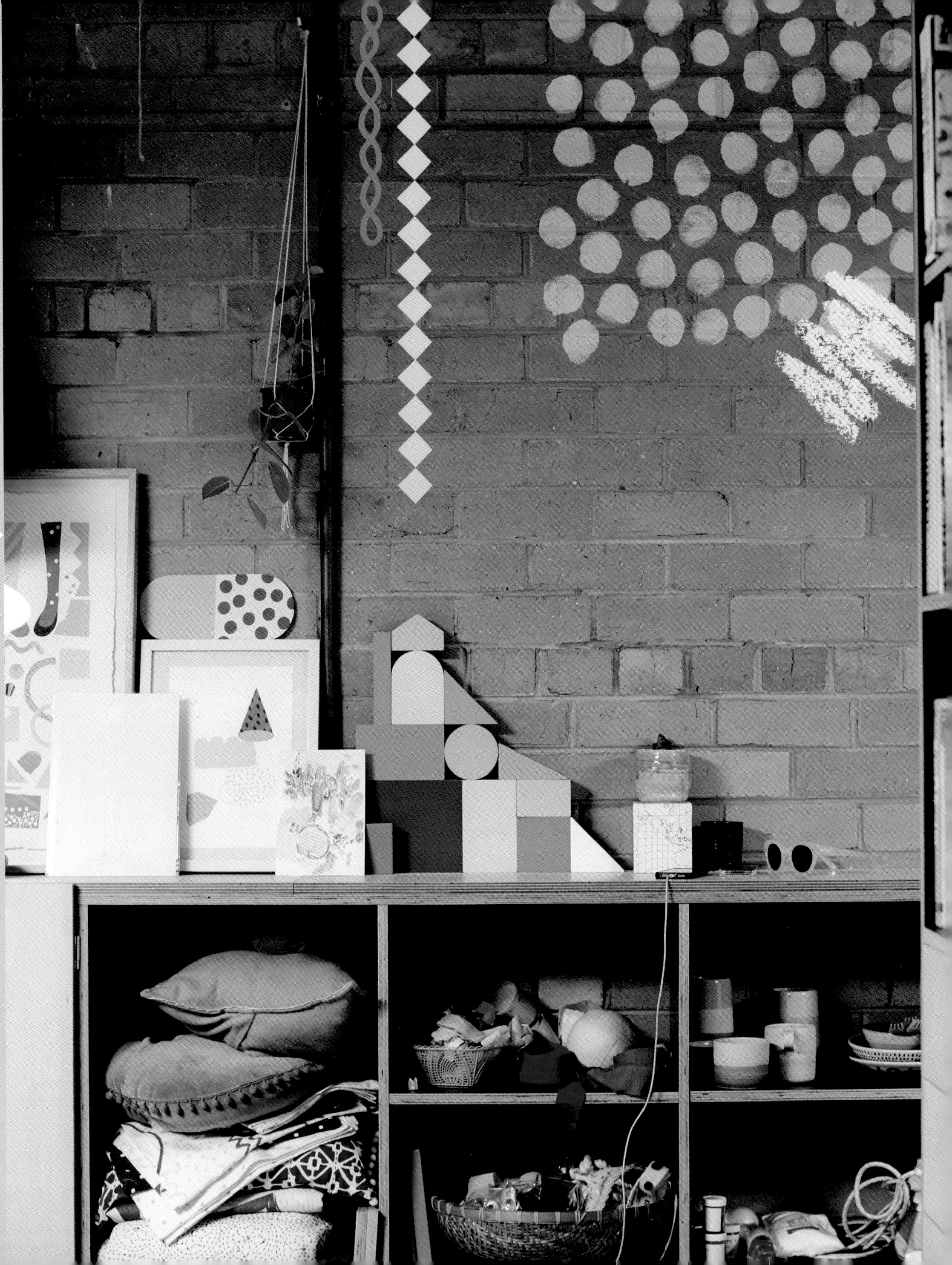

TEXTILES
PROJECTS

TEXTILE
LOVE

This chapter does include some sewing projects. Apart from a few random pieces of clothing that I've made over the years (mostly long stretchy skirts with elastic waists in my raving days), I am pretty much a sewing novice. I bought a sewing machine for my last book, and I've progressed in leaps and bounds since then. Well, maybe not leaps and bounds, but my straight lines are now much straighter. I also rediscovered the therapeutic-ness of hand stitching while making some of these projects. Craft warning: I loved it so much I haven't stopped since. This could happen to you, too!

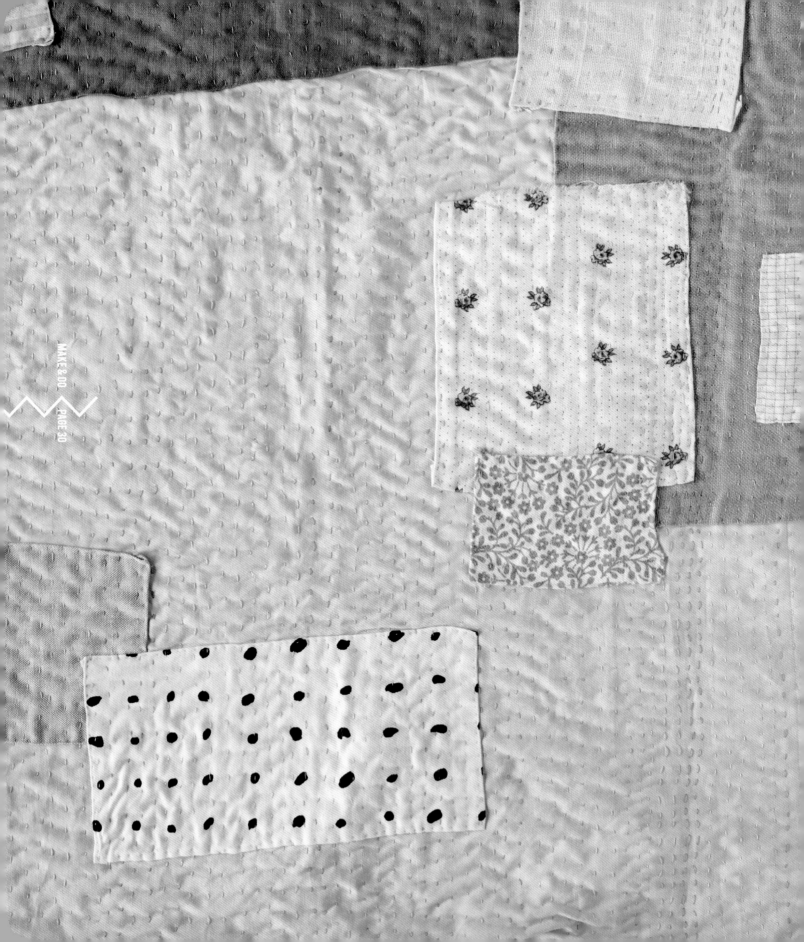

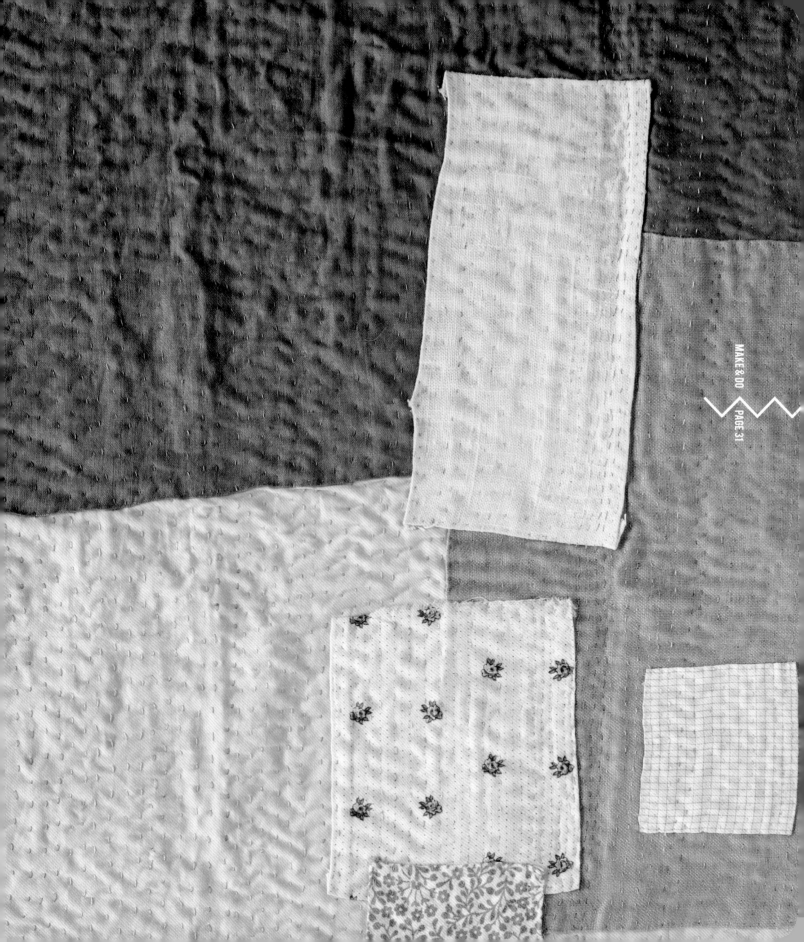

PATCHED TOTE BAG

You will need

* fabric:

  4 pieces fabric for outer, approximately 35 x 45 cm (13¾ x 17¾ in) each, including seam allowance

  4 pieces fabric for lining (use the same fabric as for the outer, or a contrasting colour)

  1 piece fabric for bottom (I used velvet), approximately 35 cm (13¾ in) square

  1 piece fabric for bottom lining, approximately 35 cm (13¾ in) square

  stiff interfacing, for bottom piece only

* Patched Tote Bag templates (page 235)

* scissors

* iron

* sewing machine and thread

* pencil

* 16 x 12 mm (½ in) gold rivets

* hammer

* 2 m (2 yd) of 1 cm (½ in) natural rope (size no. 7), cut in half

Among my many obsessions, tote bags are one of my biggest. After years of travelling to Japan (the sacred home of the tote bag), I have amassed a pretty decent collection. But there is always room for more. ALWAYS.

I wanted this bag to go with lots of outfits, so I designed it with only a few different (yet subtle) colours – and I couldn't resist a touch of gingham check, too! But the best part of this tote bag is the lush, mustard yellow velvet bottom panel. Or perhaps it's the rope handles I like the best … it's too hard to choose! Either way, I am really pleased with how it turned out, and I can see it becoming a firm favourite.

Adding the rivets takes quite a bit of trial and error, and muscle-power too, so I suggest giving it a few practice shots first, before adding them to your final bag. These rivets are bigger than the ones you usually find in craft stores. I bought them online, but they should be available at camping stores, as part of tent repair kits.

DIFFICULTY (HARD)

LET'S GO

1/

Following the templates, cut out all the fabric pieces as indicated.

2/

Iron the interfacing onto the wrong side of the bottom piece.

3/

Sew the long edges of the outer fabric pieces together to create one large piece, then sew the two long edges together to make a tube. Repeat with the lining fabric pieces.

3/

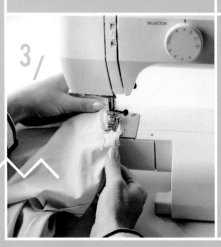

4/

Iron all the seams open.

5/

With right sides facing together, pin and then sew the bottom outer piece to the outer fabric tube. Make small cuts around the bottom piece to make this easier to manipulate (less tucks will be needed).

6/

Repeat with the lining and bottom lining pieces, but leave a 10 cm (4 in) gap when sewing, so you can turn the fabric the right way out later.

5/

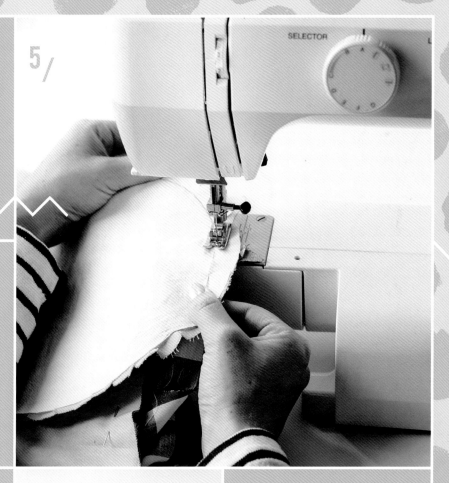

7/

Turn the outer fabric right way out. Place the outer fabric inside the lining so that the right sides are facing. Sew the top seam.

8/

Pull the outer fabric through the hole left in the bottom of the lining. Iron the top seam.

9 /

Using a pencil, mark small dots where the rivets are to be inserted. I positioned them on either side of the seams and two in between each seam (four rivets per panel).

10 /

Cut small holes in the marked spots, so that the inner cylinder of the rivet can fit through.

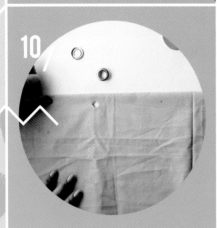

11 /

Hammer the rivets into position. Do this on a hard surface. Sew up the bottom of the lining.

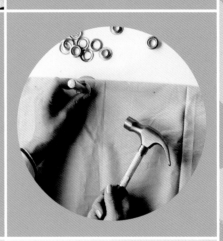

12 /

Thread the rope through the rivets. Thread one piece of rope through one side of the bag and one piece through the other side, fastening each end with a knot.

KANTHA PATCHED CUSHION

You will need

* fabric for front (I used two main panels for the front and lots of scraps for the patches)
* fabric for back
* iron
* pins
* needle
* thread (I used pale pink, pale blue, pink and gold)
* sewing machine and thread
* cushion stuffing

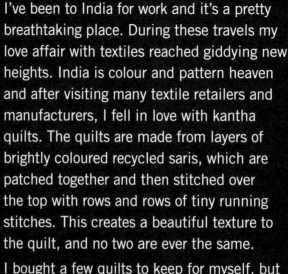

I've been to India for work and it's a pretty breathtaking place. During these travels my love affair with textiles reached giddying new heights. India is colour and pattern heaven and after visiting many textile retailers and manufacturers, I fell in love with kantha quilts. The quilts are made from layers of brightly coloured recycled saris, which are patched together and then stitched over the top with rows and rows of tiny running stitches. This creates a beautiful texture to the quilt, and no two are ever the same.

I bought a few quilts to keep for myself, but that wasn't enough to satisfy my obsession, so I started patching together some scraps of fabric to make my own. Perhaps I was blindly optimistic, but I didn't realise how time-consuming it would be. It wasn't long before the project was downsized to a cushion.

NOTE / My finished cushion is approximately 50 cm (19¾ in) square; make your cushion any size, to suit whatever fabric scraps you have.

DIFFICULTY
(MEDIUM)

LET'S GO

1/

Arrange your background fabric panels and fabric patches on a flat surface.

2/

Move the fabric pieces around until you are happy with the composition.

TIP / Take a photo of the arrangement on your phone, to use as a visual reference.

3/

Iron down the hems of each of the fabric patches.

3/

4/

Pin together the two main fabric panels for the front. Sew the two pieces together using a tiny running stitch.

5/

Pin the patches in place on top of the front panels. Sew the patches in place with running stitch.

5/

6/

Once all the patches are sewn in position, start sewing rows of running stitch over the whole panel. Stitch several rows using one colour of thread, then change the thread colour and sew several more rows. Continue in this manner, alternating the thread colour.

TIP /

Don't worry if the stitches aren't straight, it's the wonkiness that makes it beautiful.

7/

Push the needle in and out of the fabric several times before pulling the thread through. This speeds up the stitching process a little and also produces a nice texture.

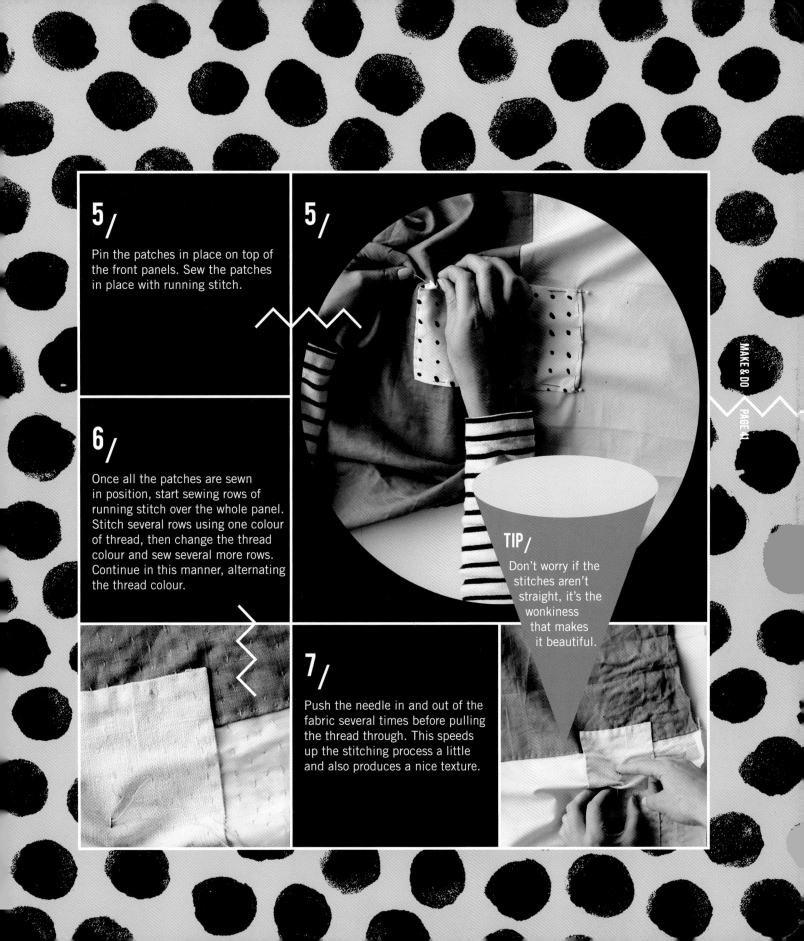

8/

Cut the back panel to size. Pin the right sides together and sew a seam 1.5 cm (½ in) from the edge on a sewing machine. Leave an opening of about 10 cm (4 in) on one side for the stuffing.

8/

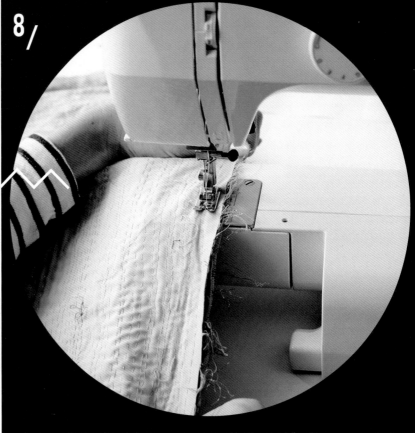

9/

Remove the pins and turn the cushion cover right sides out. Add the stuffing.

10/

Pin the open hole together, turning the edges of the fabric under, then close the hole with hand stitching.

SHIRTLESS COLLARS

You will need

* shirt with a collar you like
* scissors
* pins
* sewing machine and thread

Embroidered collar

* Shirtless Collar template (page 235)
* embroidery thread: pale pink, blue and gold
* embroidery needle
* covered button (I used a yellow button)

Pompom collar

* small pompoms
* pencil
* needle
* cotton thread, to match pompoms
* 40 cm (15¾ in) length of matching ribbon, about 1 cm (½ in) wide

Braid and beads collar

* 50 cm (19¾ in) length of braided trim
* small beads
* needle
* cotton thread, to match beads

If I had to choose one signature look for myself it would definitely involve a Peter Pan collar. I love it so much that when I found a shirt with the most perfectly shaped Peter Pan collar, I bought three of them, in different colours. I still have them, and when the sad day comes that they can no longer be worn, I'll have a pattern made so I can have an endless supply. No kidding. This is a serious situation. I intend to wear the perfect Peter Pan collar forever.

But I also love a regular collar, preferably buttoned all the way to the top. This top-buttoning does come with a certain feeling of formality, so to get around this stiffness, I have devised this easy project. All you have to do is make a few snips with the scissors and *voilà* – a collar that you can add to just about anything. Collars worn with t-shirts look super cute and definitely lower the formality factor, too.

These collars have been embellished with pompoms, embroidery, and beads and braids, but feel free to use these as starting points and add your own creative touches.

DIFFICULTY
(EASY)

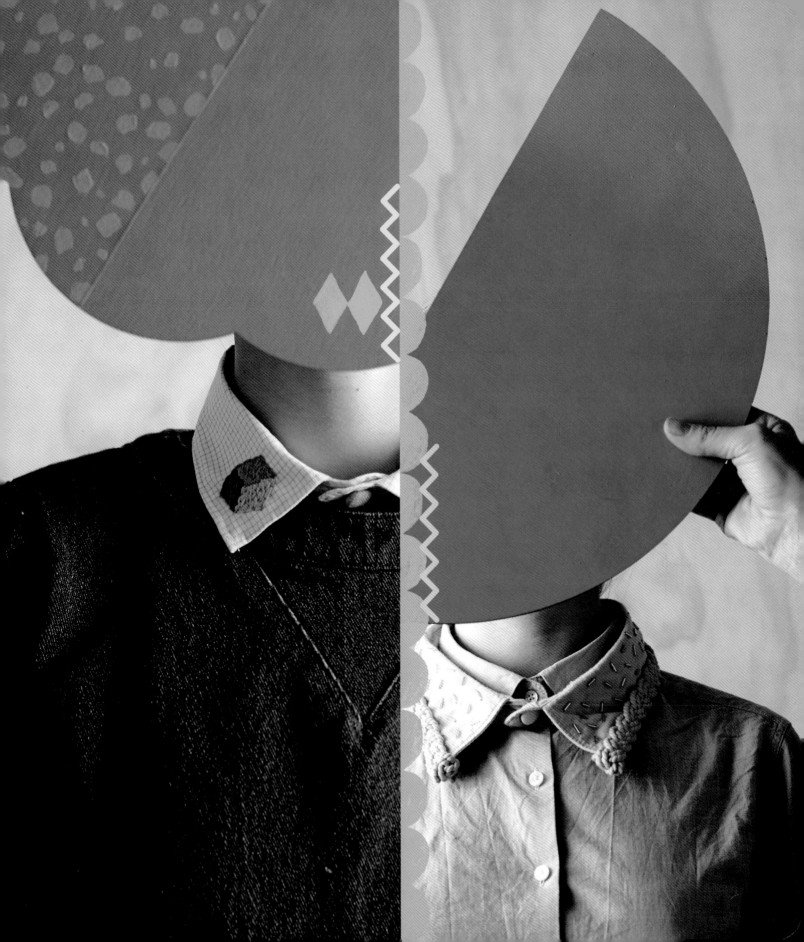

LET'S GO

1/

Cut the collar off the shirt.

2/

If you cut just under the seam of where the collar joins the shirt, then the fabric won't fray.

3/

If you are not happy with the shape of your collar, unpick the front of the collar near each corner and remove any collar stiffeners that might be included in the collar.

3/

4/

Trim the excess fabric from the collar to make the desired shape. Pin the seam and then sew it on a machine.

1/

Embroidered collar
Using the template, trace the pattern onto the collar. Use satin stitch to fill in areas of the cube and back stitch to finish off.

2/

Remove the existing button and replace it with a new button.

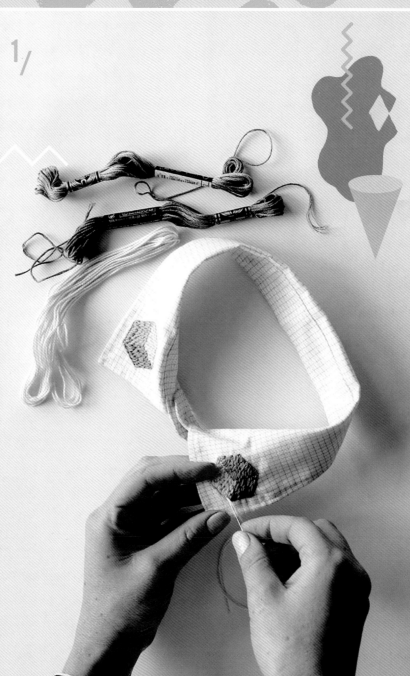

1/

Pompom collar
Arrange the pompoms on the collar, marking their positions in pencil with a small dot. Sew the pompoms onto the collar using a needle and matching thread.

2/

Cut the ribbon in half. Place the end of one ribbon under the collar, past the button hole, and hand sew it in place. Place the other ribbon half on the other side of the collar and sew it in place.

1/

1/

Braid and beads collar
Pin the braid around the edge of the collar, then sew it into place. Fold the ends of the braid under the edges of the front of the collar, and sew into place.

2/

Using a needle and matching thread, sew the small beads onto the collar, spacing them evenly apart around the collar.

BATIK FUROSHIKI

You will need

* 65 cm (25½ in) square piece fabric (I used cotton voile): washed, dried and ironed
* HB pencil
* batik wax
* heatproof container
* electric frying pan
* newspaper
* small paintbrush and/or tjanting (this is a special tool used for batik)
* black liquid cold-water dye
* large container or pot for dye
* disposable rubber gloves
* plain paper
* iron
* sewing machine and thread

I've been lucky enough to have travelled to both Malaysia and Japan, and have fallen in love with both places. This project combines two of my favourite things from those countries: batik and *furoshiki*.

On my first trip to Japan I discovered *furoshiki*, a beautiful piece of fabric used for wrapping absolutely anything – gifts, bottles and food. Even the numerous ways in which the cloth can be wrapped is a complete art in itself. In Malaysia, on one of my many visits to the local craft centres, I had the chance to watch some amazing batik artists at work. I was so inspired by what I'd seen that I knew I had to try it when I got home.

After much trial and error the main thing I learnt was that part of the beauty of batik lies in the mistakes. As an amateur batik-er, I found that the hot wax was a hard medium to control, so with that in mind, I designed the pattern for this project to be fairly random and ready to cope with any extra dots and splashes that undoubtedly would occur. When my batik was finished, it was actually the mistakes that I loved the most. Embrace the imperfections!

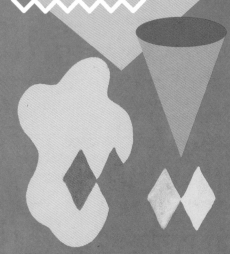

DIFFICULTY
(HARD)

LET'S GO

1/

Using the photograph on page 51 as a guide, draw the pattern onto the fabric using a lead pencil.

TIP/ Using a thin fabric such as voile will allow the wax to be fully absorbed through the material.

2/

Put the wax in a saucepan or heatproof container and place it in an electric frying pan filled with boiling water. An electric frying pan is ideal because it regulates the heat well, but you could also use a double boiler.

3/

Place the fabric on a few sheets of newspaper. When the wax has completely melted, paint the wax onto the design using either a small paintbrush or a special batik tool called a tjanting.

4/

Make sure the wax has absorbed through the fabric to the other side. If it hasn't, you may not have enough wax on your paintbrush, or you're not applying it fast enough and it may be drying on the brush.

5/

While the wax is drying, mix up the dye following the manufacturer's instructions. Wearing rubber gloves, place the fabric in the dye. Leave in the dye for the time specified in the instructions (timing will vary between brands).

6/

Remove the fabric from the dye and rinse it thoroughly under cold water. Hang it out to dry. When the fabric is dry, place it on a few sheets of newspaper.

TIP/

For tips on how to use your *furoshiki* cloth see page 232.

7/

To remove the wax from the fabric, place a piece of paper on the waxed side of the fabric and iron over it with a hot iron. The heat from the iron will melt the wax onto the paper. When you have removed all the wax, iron the fabric to set the dye. Iron down the edges and sew a hem.

CANVAS BASKETS

You can fill these baskets with just about anything, provided it's not overly liquidy. We've gone for plants here – my studio has a tendency to be pretty jungle-like and I was looking for a patterned storage alternative to the usual terracotta and plastic options. I've also used these baskets for toys, wool and even a luxe rubbish bin.

The baskets are easy to make, so if you have never sewn before then this would be a perfect start – plus you get the fun and satisfaction of stamping your own pattern on the fabrics beforehand.

DIFFICULTY
(MEDIUM)

You will need

* uncut rubber stamp
* stamp cutting tools
* fabric stamping ink
* fabric:
  46 x 86 cm (18 x 33¾ in) for larger basket; 33 x 57 cm (13 x 22½ in) for smaller basket

  For 1 basket (of your chosen size) you will need:

  1 piece fabric for outer (a heavier weight fabric such as canvas is ideal)

  1 piece fabric for lining

  1 piece of stiff interfacing
* scissors
* iron
* sewing machine and thread
* ruler

Mix and match the
fabric lining and
outer patterns

LET'S GO

1/

Using the uncut stamp and your cutting tools, cut out the stamp. I used a circle, a square and an asterisks shape.

TIP / Test your stamp on a piece of scrap fabric to see how it looks.

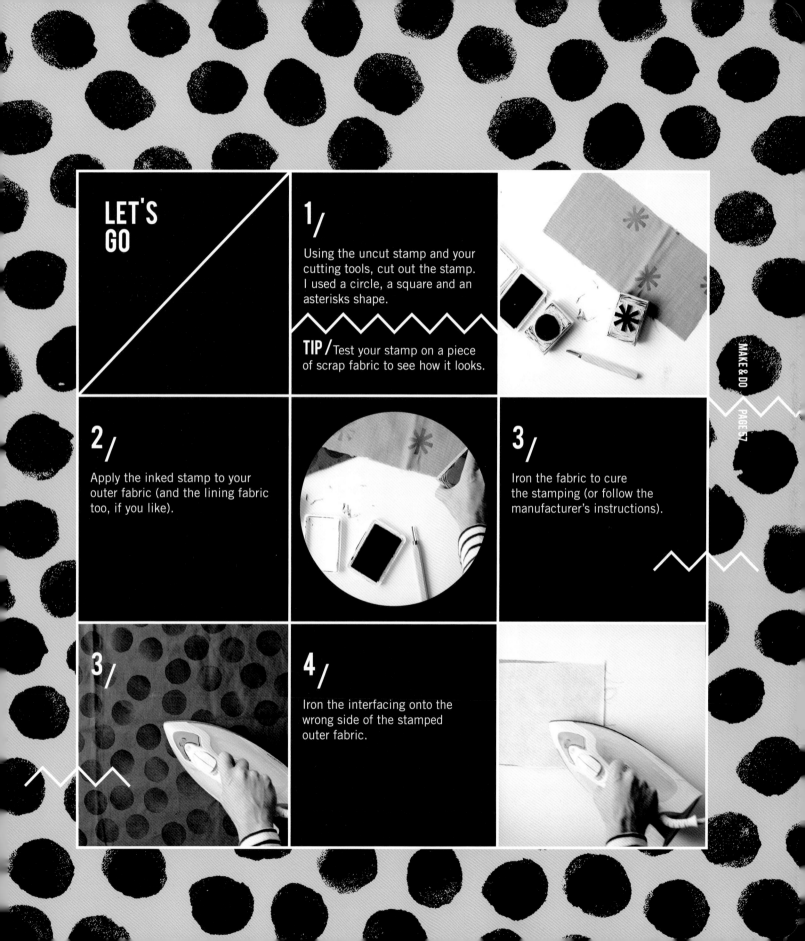

2/

Apply the inked stamp to your outer fabric (and the lining fabric too, if you like).

3/

Iron the fabric to cure the stamping (or follow the manufacturer's instructions).

3/

4/

Iron the interfacing onto the wrong side of the stamped outer fabric.

5/

Fold the outer fabric in half widthwise, as per the diagram. Sew the two side seams. Repeat for the lining fabric.

FOLD

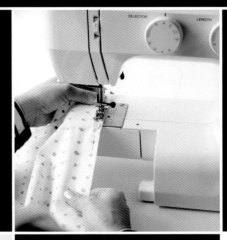

6/

Iron the seams flat on both the outer and lining fabrics.

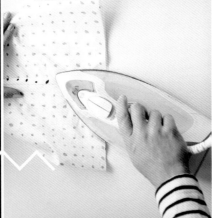

7/

Open up the bottom of the outer fabric to form a diamond. Draw up triangles on both sides of the diamond. Repeat for the lining fabric.

8/

Take the outer fabric and sew along the two drawn lines, then cut off the excess fabric, leaving a seam allowance.

9/

Repeat step 8 for the lining fabric, but leave one corner unsewn (so you can turn it right way out later).

10 /

Turn the outside fabric so the right way is facing out. Place this piece inside the lining. Both pieces should have right sides facing inwards.

11 /

Sew both pieces together around the top. Pull the outer fabric through the unsewn corner of the lining.

12 /

Sew the remaining corner of the lining.

13 /

Pull the basket into shape and fold over the top seam to show the lining.

LATCH HOOK RUG

You will need

* Latch Hook Rug template (page 234)
* 75 x 100 cm (29½ x 39½ in) piece of latch hook canvas
* thick black felt-tipped marker
* thick cardboard
* scissors
* wool:
  9–10 balls of 14 ply blue, for the background
  2 balls peach
  1 ball of each of the following: lilac, mustard, dark green, green, teal, navy, pale pink, white, grey, silver grey
* latch hook
* pins
* needle and thread

You can't get more 1970s craft than a latch hook rug. I have fond memories of latch-hooked projects displayed on walls, resplendent in their brown, orange and cream colour palettes.

When I was researching some ideas for this project, nearly all the finished pieces that I saw were of quaint country houses, floral arrangements and the occasional buxom lady (one was even lounging across a stag). I did spot some great geometric gems, but I knew a latch hook rug had more potential than that.

So I set forth to bring the latch hook into the current century, using a design that included an all-seeing eye and some of my favourite shapes. I'm so happy with the result.

A word of warning: this is definitely the longest project I have ever undertaken. Two of us worked on this for three weeks, and it was still a struggle to get it finished in time. Most likely you won't have a deadline like we did, so take your time and enjoy it. You will find you're hooked in no time (sorry, couldn't resist).

NOTE / 14 ply wool seemed to be the perfect thickness for most areas. If the ply is too thin, you have to add double stitches; if the ply is too thick, then the stitches will fall out easily.

DIFFICULTY
(MEDIUM)

LET'S GO

1/

Place the enlarged template under the latch hook canvas. Using the black marker, trace the design onto the canvas.

2/

Cut a piece of thick cardboard measuring 6.5 x 18 cm (2½ x 7 in). Fold the cardboard in half lengthwise. Wrap the wool around the cardboard to cover the length.

TIP / Using different types of yarn will create different textures.

3/

Hold the folded cardboard with the open side facing upwards, and use scissors to cut through the gap, to cut the wool into short threads.

4/

Take one piece of wool and loop it around the base of the latch hook, below the swinging latch.

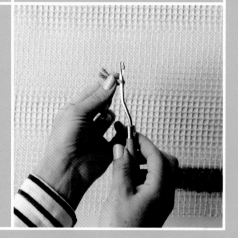

5 /

Insert the end of the hook under and then out of one canvas square (so the latch passes under one of the canvas bars). Hold the wool in place with your index finger while you do this.

6 /

Holding the two loose ends of the wool loop (make sure the ends are even), pull the loop through the top of the hook and close the latch.

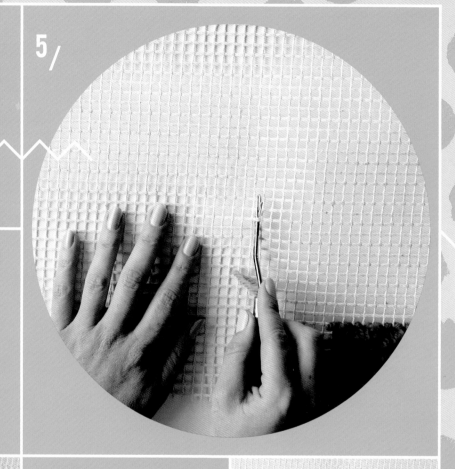

7 /

Slowly pull the hook back out and under the canvas bar. As you do this, the latch will close and the wool will attach itself to the canvas with a slip-type knot. Release the wool and pull the hook through.

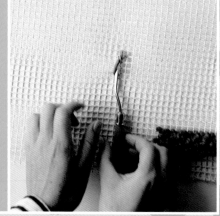

8/

Continue adding stitches until an area of colour is filled, and then move on to the next area.

8/

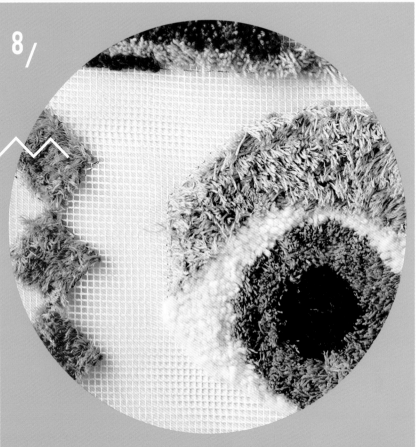

9/

When the rug is completed, turn it over and pin a 2 cm (¾ in) hem around all four sides. Stitch down the edges.

TIP/ Run a steaming iron over the back of the rug. This will help to secure the wool threads in place. You might also like to add a rubber backing so the rug won't slip.

RAINBOW SOCKS & CHECK LEGGINGS

You will need

Socks
* 1 pair long white socks
* newspaper
* fabric markers: pink, green, orange, yellow, red and blue
* small spray bottle with water
* small spray dye: we used fluoro pink and blue (these ready-made dyes are sold in small spray bottles and are available from most craft stores)
* iron

Leggings
* 1 pair white leggings
* thick cardboard
* pencil
* scissors
* newspaper
* hot-water blue dye (and fixative)
* container for dye
* disposable rubber gloves
* 3 cm (1¼ in) wide paintbrush

I had a go at playing with some dye in my first book, *Find & Keep*, and because it's something I like to do in my studio, I thought a second dye project was in order. Strictly speaking, it's only the leggings that are painted with dye; the socks are painted with fabric markers, but I figure that fabric markers are really just a less messy and more contained version of dye anyway!

Either way, both projects transform something boring and plain into something that's much more fun and wearable. As proof, the leggings have become one of my favourite things to wear.

DIFFICULTY
(MEDIUM)

LET'S GO

1/

Socks
Wet the socks thoroughly. Lay them both flat on a few sheets of newspaper.

2/

Using the fabric markers, add a few patches of colour to one of the socks.

3/

The markers will 'bleed' a little on the wet socks. Encourage the dye to spread by rubbing the fabric together.

3/

4/

As you work down the length of the sock, use the water spray bottle to spray a little water over the coloured areas, to create interesting patterns. Continue until you are happy with the amount of colour.

5/

Turn the sock over and do the same on the other side. Some of the fabric markers will have already bled through. Continue colouring in small areas with the fabric markers, and spreading the colour out by rubbing the fabric and spraying it with water.

6/

When you have finished both sides, check that the dye has been applied evenly down the sides of the sock where it has been folded flat – even the colour out if necessary.

7/

Add dye spray to the sock. These dyes are quite pigmented and will provide contrasting splashes of bright colour. Repeat the process for the second sock. When the socks are thoroughly dry, iron them to set the dye.

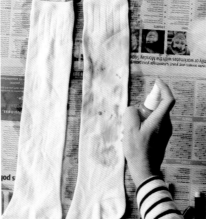

LET'S GO

1/

Leggings
Place the leggings on a piece of cardboard and draw around the leg section with a pencil. Cut out two pieces of cardboard in the shape of each leg. Insert the cardboard into the legs of the leggings to separate the front and back, to prevent the dye from bleeding through.

2/

Place the leggings on a few sheets of newspaper. Use a pencil to draw horizontal and vertical lines on the leggings, spacing the lines about 6 cm (2¼ in) apart.

3/

Mix up the dye following the manufacturer's instructions. Wearing rubber gloves and using the wide paintbrush, paint a few horizontal lines. The dye will bleed a little but that's part of the loveliness of hand painting with dye.

3/

4/

When you've added several horizontal lines, start to form checks by adding vertical lines.

TIP/ Mix up half the dye to paint the front, then the remaining for the back. The dye can lose its intensity if it's not used quickly.

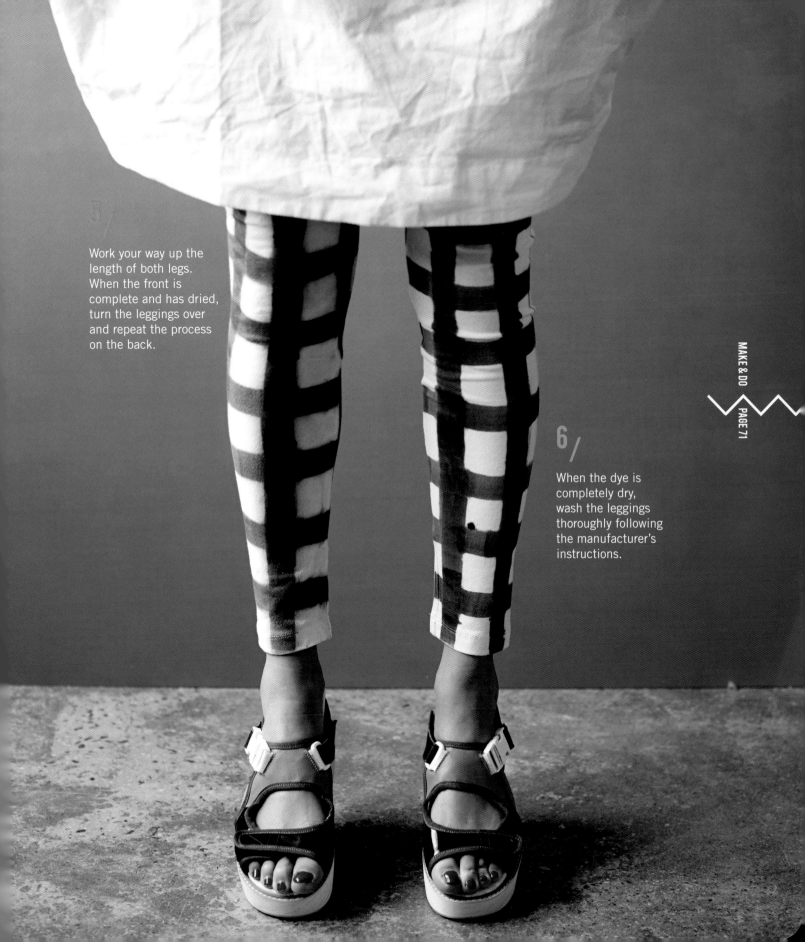

5/

Work your way up the length of both legs. When the front is complete and has dried, turn the leggings over and repeat the process on the back.

6/

When the dye is completely dry, wash the leggings thoroughly following the manufacturer's instructions.

MAKE & DO
PAGE 71

PAPER

If I had to choose one material to work with for the rest of my life it would be paper.

Paper is for everyone! It's usually the first medium you work with as a child, and for good reason. It's accessible, cheap and, above all, it's versatile. You can paint it, cut it, fold it, rip it, glue it, wrap it, draw on it, marble it ... and that's just the beginning.

My passion for working with paper (primary school collages aside) first came from wanting to transform the drawings I made on my computer into something more tactile and organic – paper had the same beautiful flatness and quality of solid colour as the graphics on my computer screen. I've gone on to work with paper in some form or other in every art exhibition I have had.

As you may know from reading my previous books, I have built up a pretty good paper collection over the years. It's all stored in colour-coded drawers in a huge plan press and is one of the pride and joys of my studio.

Recently, however, my paper collection has turned more into an obsession. I wanted to hold on to the tiniest paper scraps because I loved the colour and would I ever find that same colour again? (Most likely, yes.) Or how could I possibly throw out this scrap because look at how beautiful the shape is? (It's trash so throw it out.) I ended up with more scraps of paper than good paper and then when the drawers on my plan press would no longer close properly, I knew the situation was slightly out of control.

My solution: to make a series of collages using my most favourite paper scraps. That way they wouldn't get thrown out, and instead they would be framed forever, and if I was lucky someone else might buy them and love them forever, too. It was a good solution. The scraps that weren't used for the collages went in the bin. Well, most of them ... some I just couldn't bare to part with.

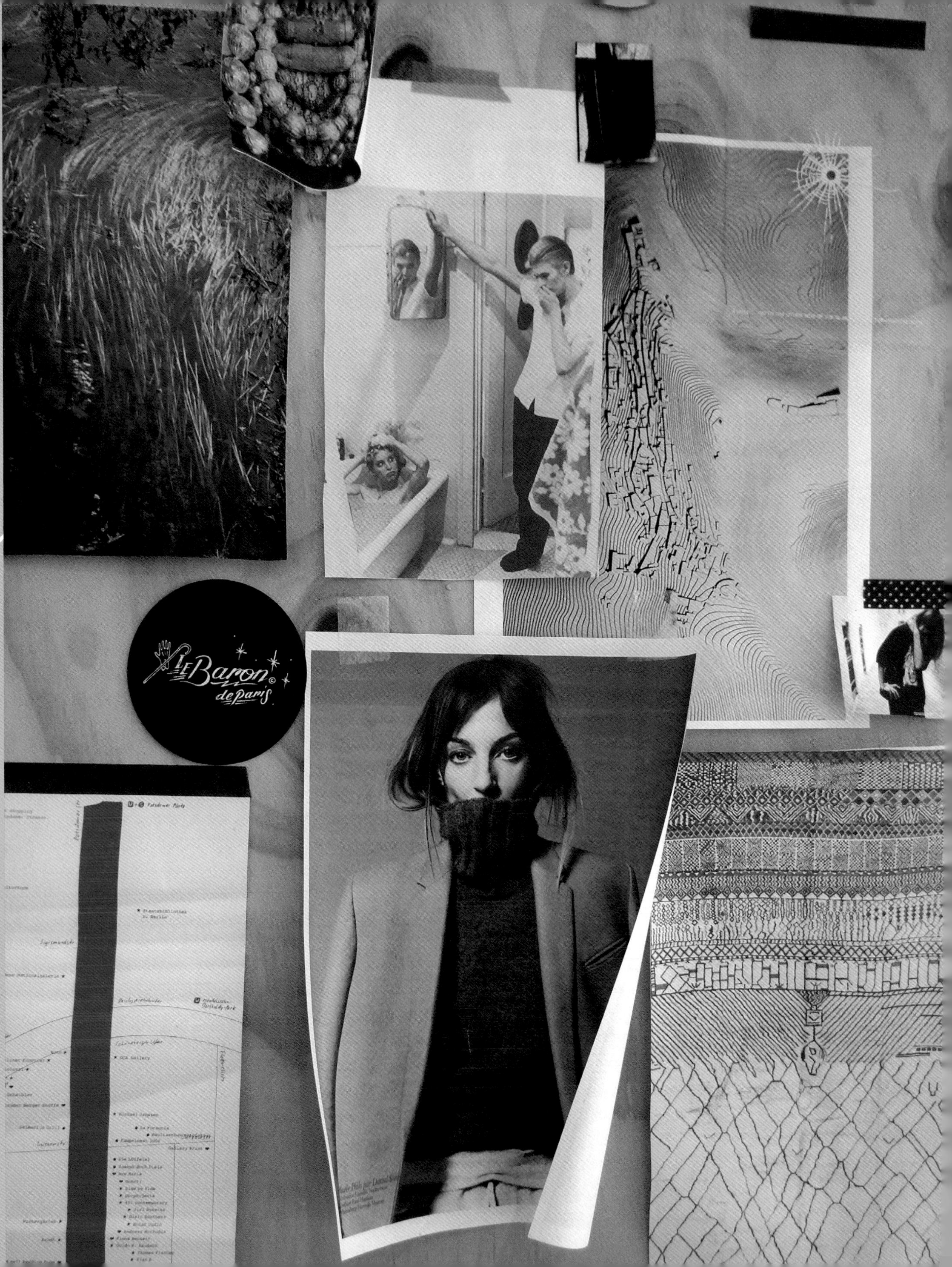
Le Baron de Paris

PAPER PROJECTS

PAPER
LOVE

When making the projects for this chapter I really got to take my love for paper to another level – paper really is a spectacular and versatile medium. My main aim was to create projects using as many different papers as I could think of: tissue paper, card, crepe – even toilet paper! I hope you will develop a love of paper while making some of these things too.

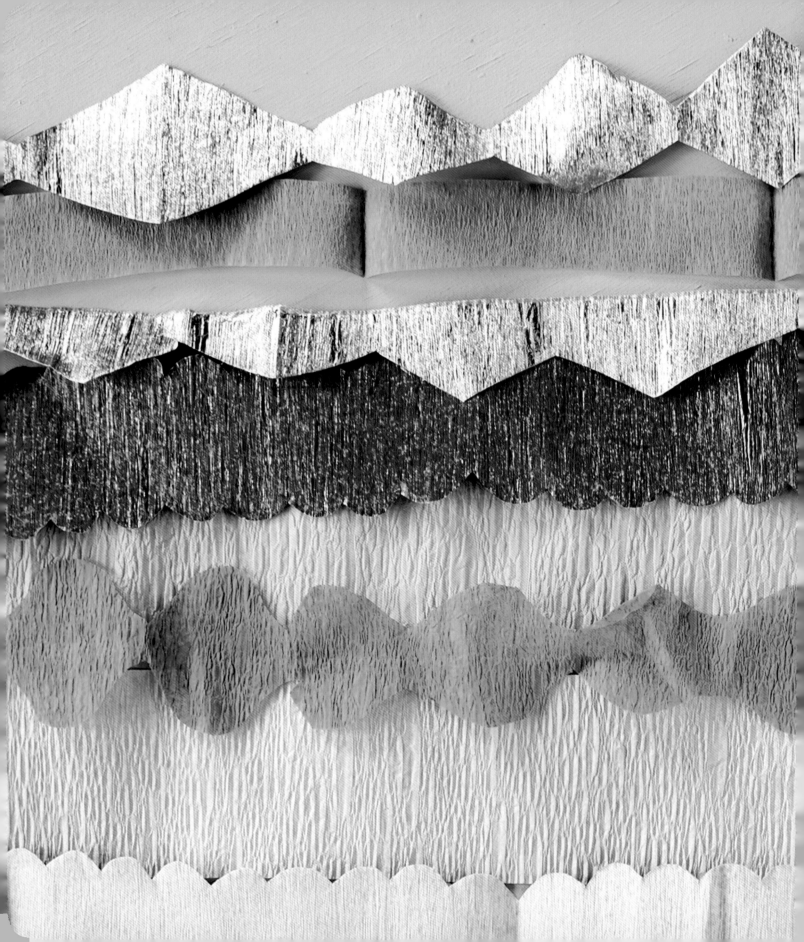

MAKE & DO
PAGE 91

PAPER CLOWN
COSTUME

You will need

* pencil
* ruler
* white tissue paper
* green tissue paper
* scissors
* glue
* paintbrushes
* 2 pieces green card, about 200 gsm, 50 x 70 cm (19¾ x 27½ in)
* 1 piece peach card, about 200 gsm, 50 x 70 cm (19¾ x 27½ in)
* double-sided tape and sticky tape
* hole punch
* hat elastic
* white paint
* 4 peach pompoms, with long strings

I'm not really one for dress-up parties. I love them in theory, but I live in fear of arriving at the party and discovering that I'm the only one dressed up. This is not an irrational fear, but one based on actual events when, at the tender age of sixteen, I went to a Halloween party dressed as a sexy French maid only to arrive and find that no one else had bothered to dress up. I wasn't ridiculed but it wasn't exactly the crowning glory of my teenage social life either.

This clown costume is a somewhat fail-safe option. It's not the whole hog, so if you do rock up to the party and find you're the only one dressed up, then it's easy enough to quickly de-costume. Or, you can wear it with pride!

NOTE / This would make a great Pierrot costume if you change the colour scheme. Make white neck and wrist ruffles, and a white hat with black pompoms.

DIFFICULTY
(MEDIUM)

LET'S GO

1/

Ruffle

Using a pencil, draw 3.5 cm (1½ in) circles onto the white and green pieces of tissue paper. (Use a cardboard template for your circle or trace around a coin or small lid.) You will need about 36 white and 60 green circles. Cut out the circles.

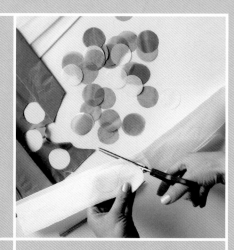

2/

Glue the white circles onto one piece of green card. Glue the green circles onto the peach card.

3/

Take the green card and with the 50 cm (19¾ in) side nearest to you, rule up three strips, each measuring 16.5 cm (6½ in) wide. Cut the strips.

3/

4/

Using double-sided tape, stick the strips end to end to form one long piece of card.

5/

Starting at one end, make concertina folds in the card, with each fold being about 6 cm (2¼ in) apart.

6/

Cut the peach card into three 8 cm (3¼ in) wide strips and repeat steps 4 and 5. (The remaining peach card will be used for the wrist ruffles.)

7/

Using the hole punch, punch holes along one side of the green card, positioning the hole in the centre of each folded section. Hold small sections of the folded card together and punch a hole through a few layers at a time. Do the same along one side of the peach card.

7/

8/

Cut a 70 cm (27½ in) piece of elastic. Place the peach card on top of the green card. Leaving a length of elastic at the start, thread the elastic through the holes of both the peach and green cards. Tie the ends of the elastic together with a bow.

9 /

Wrist ruffles
Take the peach card and cut two
3.5 x 50 cm (1½ x 19¾ in) strips.

10 /

Make concertina folds in both
cards, with each fold being about
3.5 cm (1½ in) apart. Punch
holes along one side of both
cards. Cut two 20 cm (8 in)
pieces of elastic. Thread
the elastic through the
holes and secure with a bow.

10 /

11 /

Hat
Take the remaining piece of green
card and curl it up to form a
cone. Cut the bottom off the cone
so the hat is straight.

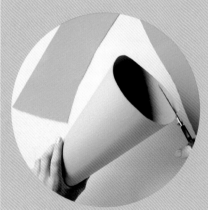

12 /

Secure the card in place with
double-sided tape or sticky tape.

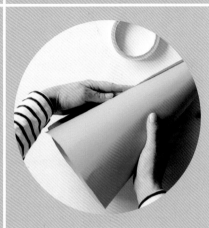

13 /

Paint some thin white stripes around the hat. Allow to dry.

14 /

Using a pencil, mark the positions for your pompoms, spacing them evenly down the front. Use the tip of your scissors to make three small holes in the hat.

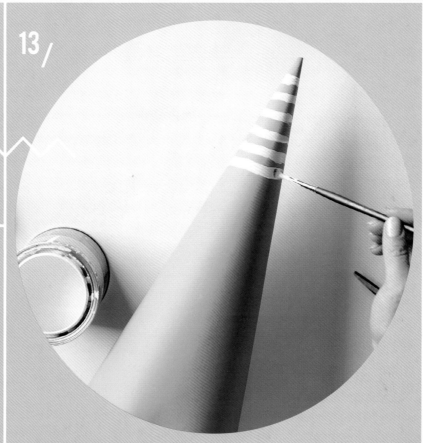

13 /

15 /

Push the pompom string into the first hole. Reach inside the hat and grab the string, then tape it to the inside of the hat. Add three pompoms to the front, and one on the top. Add a piece of elastic for a chin strap, if required.

PAPER BROOCHES

You will need

* coloured card, 220 gsm: yellow, blue, dark blue, pink, gold glitter
* pastels, acrylic paint and paintbrushes, spray paint
* Paper Brooches templates (page 233)
* scissors
* 3 mm (⅛ in) circle paper punch
* PVA glue
* string, for balloon brooch
* craft knife
* balsa wood sheets
* brooch pin backs

A few years ago, we were going to a wedding and I was running very late, madly searching for just the right accessory to break up my all-black outfit. I was working from home then, so I frantically searched through my studio, grabbed some gold glitter card and cut it into a triangle. I taped a pin on the back and, hey presto, my first paper brooch.

That brooch went on to be my favourite accessory for some time, and people often asked me where I got it from. Unfortunately, I accidentally put it through the wash and everything ended up covered in a glittery papery mess … but I simply made another one. That's the beauty of paper brooches – it's not hard to whip one up when the mood strikes or when you need something to suit a certain outfit … although they will last a bit longer if you don't put them through the wash.

These brooches are a little more complicated to make than my gold triangle brooch. I think they look best worn as a set.

DIFFICULTY
(EASY)

LET'S GO

1/

Add some pattern to the coloured card. I used pastels, acrylic paint and spray paint.

2/

Using the templates, cut out all the brooch shapes.

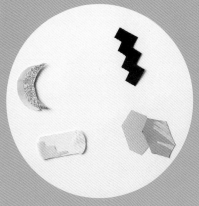

3/

Using the paper punch, punch out some small circles on the hexagon-shaped brooch.

4/

Assemble the shapes for the brooches. Glue the main shapes on top of each other, positioning them so they are slightly offset, then glue on the smaller pieces. Glue the string to the back of the balloon brooch.

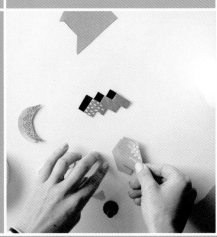

5/

Using the craft knife, cut the balsa wood into small strips, to fit the size of the brooches. Glue them to the back of the cards.

6/

Glue the brooch pin backs onto the strips of balsa wood and leave to dry.

6/

TIP/ If you like, add a coat of varnish to give your cardboard brooches better longevity.

MARBLED JOURNALS

You will need

* marbling kit: tray, paper pigment dyes, paper, comb
* other papers, such as graph, coloured or textured paper
* plain journals with spine, A5 size
* double-sided tape
* scissors
* washi tape or sticky tape

I bought my first marbling kit last year and I've had a lot of fun with it. I was really pleased with how the marbling worked on paper, but I could never find enough things to do with all the papers once I had marbled them. I made umpteen marbled paper cards and also used the paper to wrap presents, but that was it, and the thought of having to throw my favourite pieces into the bin broke my hoarder's heart a little.

Then, one day, a dream came true. Muji, the Japanese utilitarian design store, opened in my home town of Melbourne. Muji fulfils my dreams in many ways, and one of them was providing me with a plethora of plain journals. These journals, although beautiful untouched, also gave me something to wrap my marbled paper around. Now I can use and admire my marbled journals every day.

If you think you might like to invest in a marbling kit, then note that you can use the dyes on silk as well.

DIFFICULTY
(MEDIUM)

LET'S GO

1/

Pour some water into the marbling tray.

2/

Add the dyes to the paper dots (included in the marbling kit) and swirl to mix.

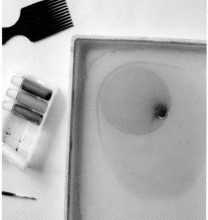

3/

Gently swirl the dyes around until you are happy with your marbling pattern. Using different objects to swirl the dye will produce different patterns.

3/

4/

Carefully lay a piece of paper on top of the water to soak up the dye. Immediately remove the paper – don't let the paper sink into the water. Repeat three or four times, or until the dye becomes too faint to see.

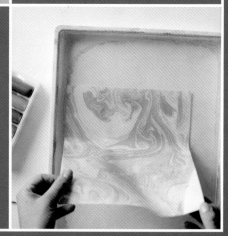

5 /

Set the papers out to dry, either pegged on a line or laying flat on a table.

6 /

Lay a piece of dry marbled paper on the table, marbled side down, and place a journal on the top. If necessary, trim the paper to fit the journal, leaving enough paper for folding.

5 /

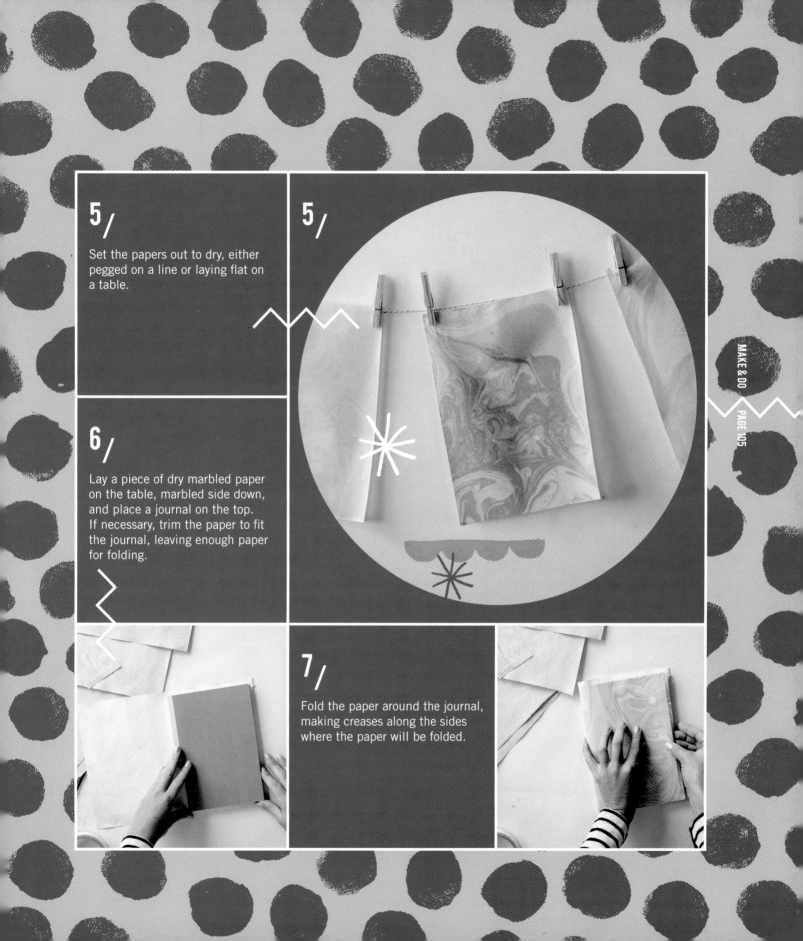

7 /

Fold the paper around the journal, making creases along the sides where the paper will be folded.

8/

Add pieces of double-sided tape to the front of the journal. When all the tape is in place, peel off the paper backings to expose the adhesive.

9/

Fold the paper onto the front of the book, smoothing it down to adhere to the tape. Turn the journal over and do the same on the back.

10/

Using scissors, cut off the excess paper on each of the four corners.

10/

11/

Fold the paper over to the inside front cover and secure it in place with washi tape or sticky tape. Do the same for the back cover.

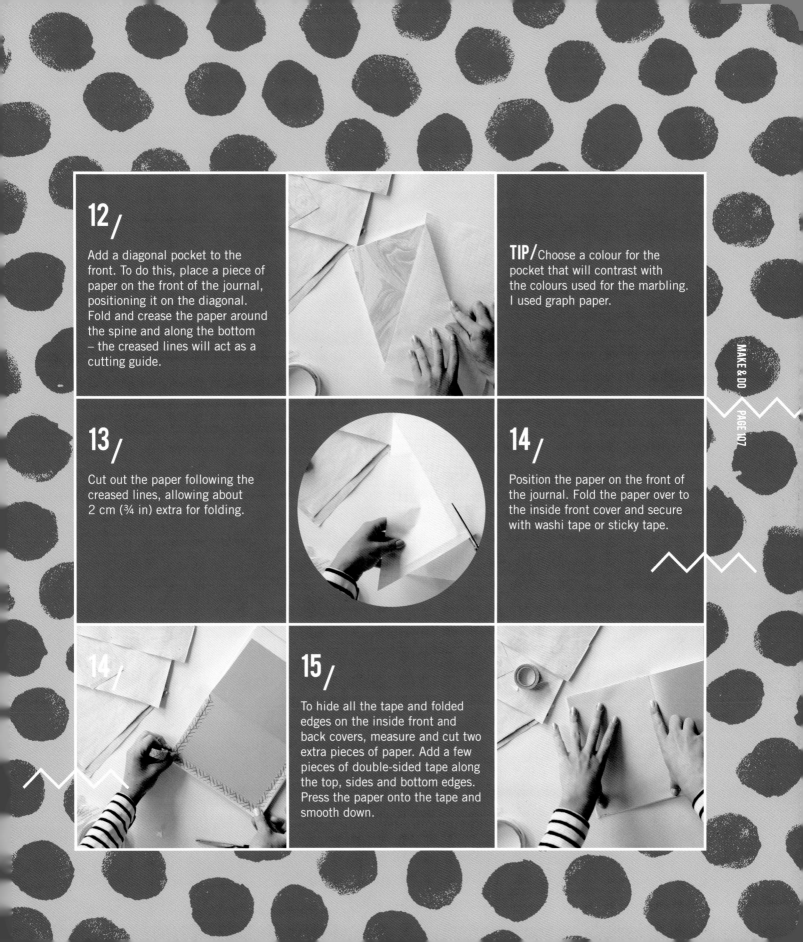

12 /

Add a diagonal pocket to the front. To do this, place a piece of paper on the front of the journal, positioning it on the diagonal. Fold and crease the paper around the spine and along the bottom – the creased lines will act as a cutting guide.

TIP/ Choose a colour for the pocket that will contrast with the colours used for the marbling. I used graph paper.

13 /

Cut out the paper following the creased lines, allowing about 2 cm (¾ in) extra for folding.

14 /

Position the paper on the front of the journal. Fold the paper over to the inside front cover and secure with washi tape or sticky tape.

14 /

15 /

To hide all the tape and folded edges on the inside front and back covers, measure and cut two extra pieces of paper. Add a few pieces of double-sided tape along the top, sides and bottom edges. Press the paper onto the tape and smooth down.

SURPRISE BALL

You will need

* small toys or gifts (I used 10)
* 4–5 rolls of crepe paper streamers in assorted colours, about 4 cm (1½ in) wide, or 8 sheets of crepe paper, cut into 4 cm (1½ in) wide strips
* PVA glue
* spray paint
* metallic crepe: red, gold, blue
* scissors
* Surprise Ball template (page 235) or 2 large ready-made stickers, for top and bottom

Raph brought me home a surprise ball one day. This ball was a special one because it was created by the very talented Gina Namkung, and was made with layers of perfectly coloured crepe paper and filled with beautifully considered vintage bits and pieces. I was feeling pretty grumpy that day, so it was a great surprise even before I opened it. This project was inspired by that gift – thank you Raph and Gina.

I think part of the whole enjoyment in making these surprise balls is searching for all the cute things to go inside it. This one contains a healthy mix of eBay, flea market and op shop finds. And then, of course, there's the fun of wrapping up your collection of goodies and giving it to someone. To make it even more special, try to include a few gifts that would really mean something to the person you are giving it to.

There's a few of my own touches added to this surprise ball. I've spray-painted some of the streamers and added some patterned strips and seals, which I cut from metallic crepe paper.

DIFFICULTY
(MEDIUM)

LET'S GO

1/

Select your first gift and wrap it in a crepe streamer.

2/

Continue wrapping the streamer around the gift until the item is completely covered, keeping in mind that you need to create a round shape. Glue the end of the streamer in place.

3/

Place the second gift on top and wrap it up using a different coloured streamer. As each gift is covered, add another layer, alternating the colours of the streamers so that each layer is different from the last.

TIP/ As you add each layer, place the gift on a different side of the ball from the last one, so the shape remains as round as possible.

4 /

Once all the gifts have been added, add a final layer of wrap and secure the end with glue. My finished ball was about 15 cm (6 in) in diameter.

4 /

5 /

Using spray paint, spray some streamers and leave to dry. These will be used to decorate the ball.

6 /

Cut out strips in various shapes from the metallic crepe paper.

7/

Decorate the ball by adding some strips of coloured crepe, the spray-painted crepe and the metallic crepe around the outside. Secure in place with glue.

8/

To complete the ball, use the template to cut out two seals from the metallic crepe. Glue them in place on the top and bottom of the ball. This will add the finishing touches to your surprise ball and will also hold all the strips in place. If preferred, use ready-made stickers instead.

PAPIER MÂCHÉ TAXIDERMY

You will need

* Papier Mâché Animals base templates (page 237)
* cardboard (I used cardboard boxes)
* scissors
* newspaper
* masking tape
* PVA glue
* plastic container or bucket for glue
* toilet paper or white tissue paper
* pencil
* acrylic paint
* paintbrushes

One of my studio helpers, Esther, introduced me to a new and easier way of making papier mâché. Instead of wrestling with wire for the base and strips of newspaper to go over it, you simply mould the base using scrunched paper, hold it in place with masking tape and then add squares of toilet paper over the top. Apparently the cheaper the toilet paper, the better it works.

I think these 'taxidermied' guys have worked really well. Best of all, no lives were lost and no blood was shed in the making of this project (although possibly a lot of PVA glue was).

This was also a huge hit with my kids. Sadly, I've noticed that the older they get, the less crafty they've become, but they happily spent many weekends making weird papier mâché Pokemon creatures to go on the walls of their bedrooms. It's getting scary in there.

DIFFICULTY
(MEDIUM)

Have fun
displaying
your creations

LET'S GO

1/

Using the templates, cut out the base shapes from cardboard.

2/

Start to form the basic shape for the head using scrunched balls of newspaper.

3/

Add masking tape to hold the newspaper in place. Add the cardboard pieces for the ears and neck, and secure in position with masking tape.

4 /

When you are happy with the shape, cover it completely with masking tape.

5 /

Mix up the glue for the papier mâché at a ratio of one part PVA glue to one part water.

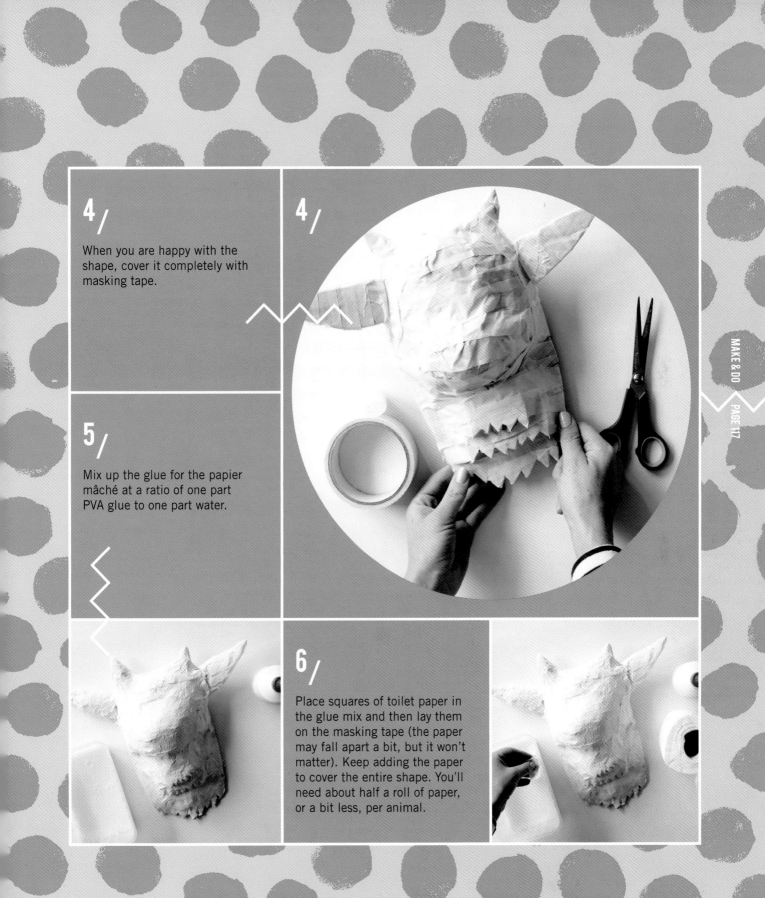

4 /

6 /

Place squares of toilet paper in the glue mix and then lay them on the masking tape (the paper may fall apart a bit, but it won't matter). Keep adding the paper to cover the entire shape. You'll need about half a roll of paper, or a bit less, per animal.

7/

Squash a few pieces of toilet paper into more defined shapes to create details such as the nose, then add a few pieces of glued paper over the top to smooth it over.

8/

Allow to dry thoroughly – this may take only a few hours or overnight. When dry, use a pencil to draw on the facial details.

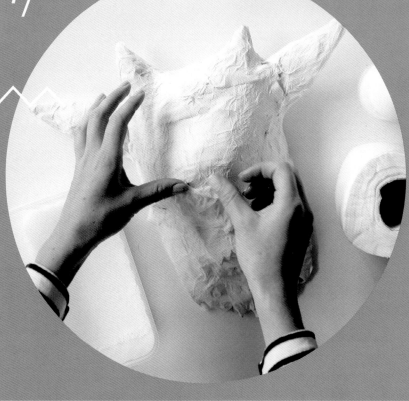

7/

9/

Using the painting guide on page 237, paint the background colour first, then use a smaller brush to add the detailed areas.

Choose your favourite animal or pet as inspiration for your papier mâché

MY FAVOURITE LYRICS

You will need

* acrylic paint: blue
* paintbrushes
* coloured card, 200 gsm: navy, light blue, pink, peach, green, yellow
* scissors or craft knife
* 6 mm (¼ in) foamcore board
* PVA glue
* My Favourite Lyrics templates (page 232)
* pink paper, for flowers on cap
* small white brad (split) pins
* printout of text
* double-sided tape

Have you ever been so enamoured by a song that you can't stop thinking about it? Perhaps you need to write fan mail, or engage in a bit of casual stalking of the artist via social media? This happens to me quite a bit. I become obsessed with certain songs and their lyrics, in this case, 'I Break Horses' by Smog (AKA Bill Callahan), which is where the text for this project comes from.

Although my musical preferences tend towards electronic music, I do venture into all genres. This song had such visual lyrics, and although the overall sentiment is a bit dark, this line alone can mean many different things. These lyrics are pretty magical to me, so I wanted to make a poster to hang on the wall so I could be constantly reminded of them.

Use this project as inspiration only. Choose your favourite lyrics and base your artwork around the words, theme or whatever part of the song inspires you.

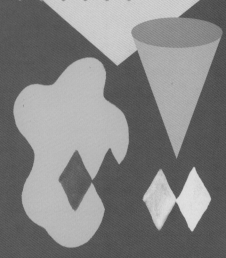

DIFFICULTY
(MEDIUM)

LET'S GO

1/

Using blue paint and a small paintbrush, paint squiggly lines on the navy card to represent waves. Cut the card into a 39 cm (15 in) circle. Cut a square piece of foamcore and glue it on the back of the circle.

2/

To make the bathing suit, paint some blue dots on a small piece of pink card.

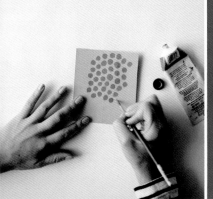

3/

Following the templates, cut out all the shapes.

3

4/

Glue small pink flowers to the blue bathing cap. To do this, add a dot of glue to the bathing cap and place the flower on the glue. When the glue has dried, carefully fold the ends of the petals up. Glue the cap to the head.

5/

Secure the two legs to the bathing suit with a brad pin. Pin the top half of the movable arm to the bottom half of the arm with a brad pin. Glue this arm to the top of the bathing suit. Glue the head onto the bathing suit, then attach the bottom arm to the neck using a brad pin.

5/

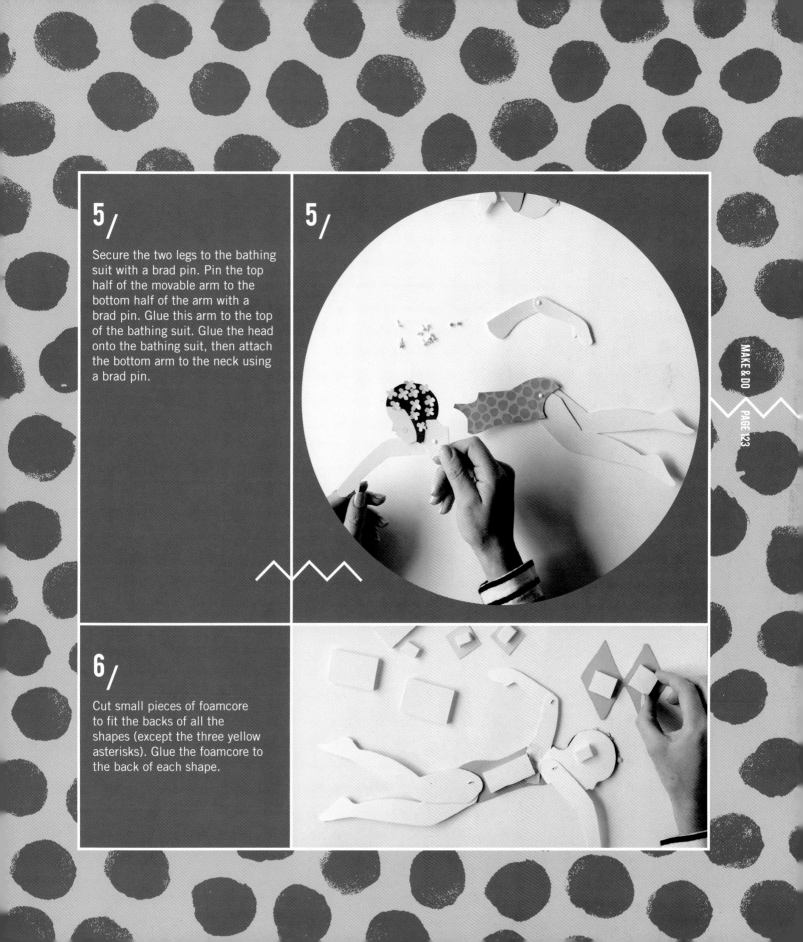

6/

Cut small pieces of foamcore to fit the backs of all the shapes (except the three yellow asterisks). Glue the foamcore to the back of each shape.

7 /

Following the template, cut out the piece of paper with the lyrics.

8 /

Assemble the lyrics and shapes on the navy background. Use glue or double-sided tape to stick the shapes into place. Add the completed swimmer last.

8 /

TONIGHT I'M SWIMMING TO MY FAVOURITE ISLAND

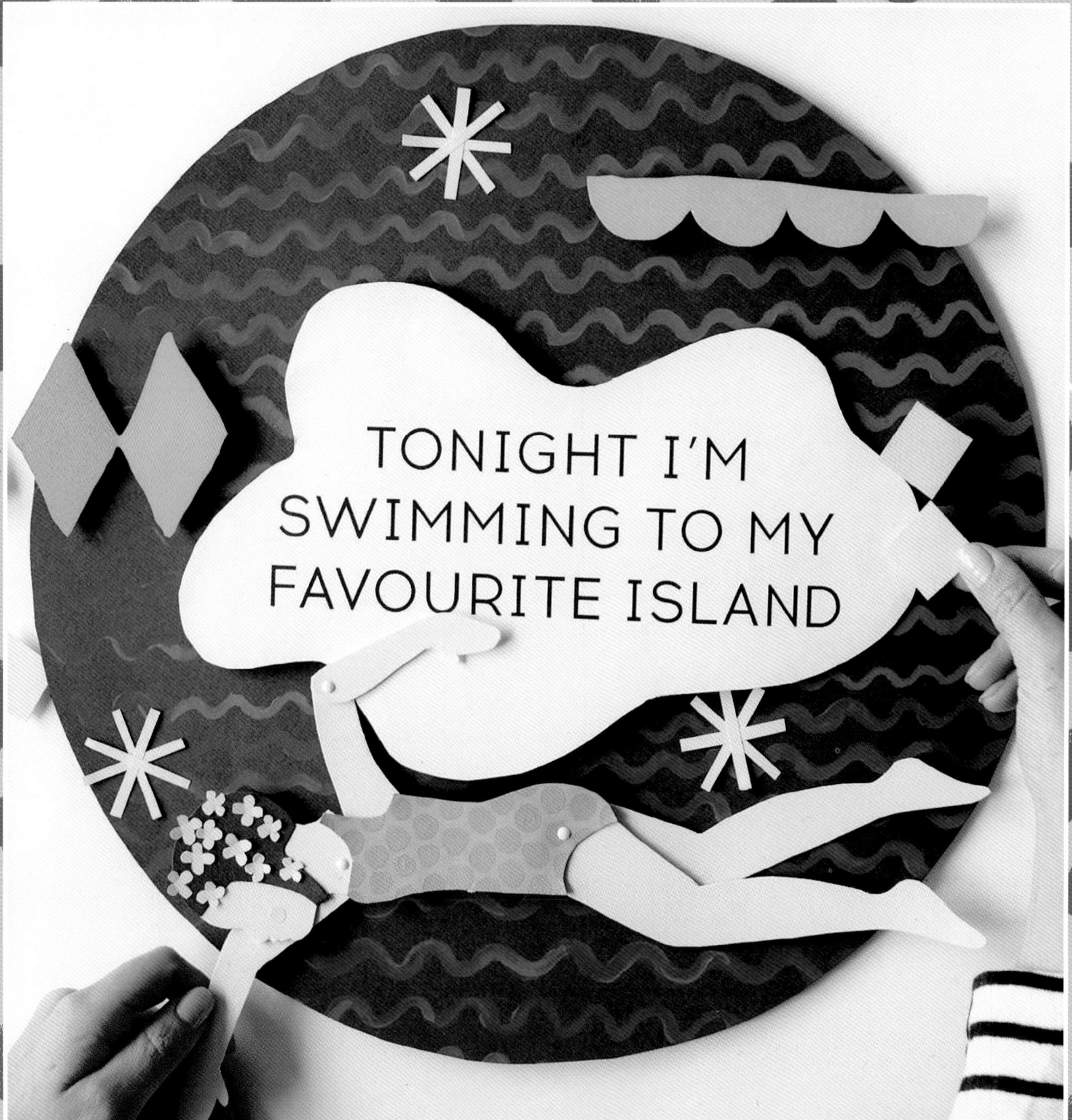
TONIGHT I'M
SWIMMING TO MY
FAVOURITE ISLAND

PAPER LANTERNS

You will need

* tissue paper in various colours, for shapes and tassels
* scissors
* paper lanterns, white or assorted colours: 50 cm (19¾ in), 30 cm (11¾ in), 20 cm (8 in)
* glue
* paintbrush
* spray paint
* sticky tape
* string
* wooden beads

Raph and I love to throw a party. We are born hosts you might say. My preference is for really big parties with all the trimmings – food, fancy drinks, lights and decorations. I try not to go too over the top so the occasion doesn't feel too formal, but it's the smaller details that make it extra special – things that your guests usually don't really notice. That's the trick to a good party, I think.

These paper lanterns are a great party trimming. Super easy, inexpensive and quick to make, the lanterns look great when hung en masse, with all parts colour co-ordinated, too.

DIFFICULTY
(EASY)

LET'S
GO

1/

Paper shapes
Cut out various shapes from the tissue paper, such as small squares, thin strips and small circles.

TIP/ I used paper confetti for the small circles.

2/

Assemble the large and medium paper lanterns. Glue the tissue shapes over the lanterns and leave to dry. I decorated the large lantern with squares and strips, and the medium lantern with multi-coloured dots (confetti).

3/

Spray paint
Assemble the small paper lantern. Working from the top of the lantern, apply the spray paint around the opening of the lantern and down the side a little.

3/

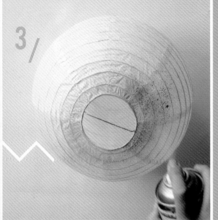

4/

Darken the colour by applying a second coat of paint. When the paint is dry, turn the lantern upside down and spray the other end the same colour, or use a contrasting colour.

5 /

For the tassels
Fold a piece of tissue paper in half and cut out a rectangle measuring about 6 x 20 cm (2¼ x 8 in). Using scissors, cut slits along the 20 cm (8 in) side of the paper, spacing the cuts about 5 mm (¼ in) apart.

6 /

Roll the paper up to form a tassel.

MAKE & DO
PAGE 130

7/

Secure the top of the tassel with sticky tape.

8/

Place a small length of string at the top of the tassel and secure with another piece of tape. Thread the string through the bead, so the tassel sits at the bottom of the bead. Secure in place with glue, if required.

9/

Repeat steps 5 to 8 to make a second tassel. Tie the beaded tassels to the bottom of the small and medium lanterns. Use a piece of string to tie the small lantern to the bottom of the large lantern.

MAKE & DO

PAGE 134

My dad is a carpenter, so I grew up with the smell of sawdust in the air.

Dad has a bad case of needing to occupy his hands at all times – and I seem to have inherited that trait too. My childhood memories are of him tinkering in his shed, working on one project or another – a wooden pot plant holder, something for one of his never-ending renovations, or something for my sister and me to play with.

When we were on school holidays, we often went to building sites with Dad. Sometimes we were lucky and he was renovating an amazing mansion, so we ran around on the tennis courts or played hide and seek in the gardens.

Other times, when the gardens weren't so fun to explore, we busied ourselves playing with the wood off-cuts he gave us. We piled them high and built houses with them, or drew faces on them and invented imaginary characters – or threw them at one another when one of us was being annoying! Perhaps it was these days spent with my dad that gave me such a love for making things with wood.

MAKE & DO PAGE 135

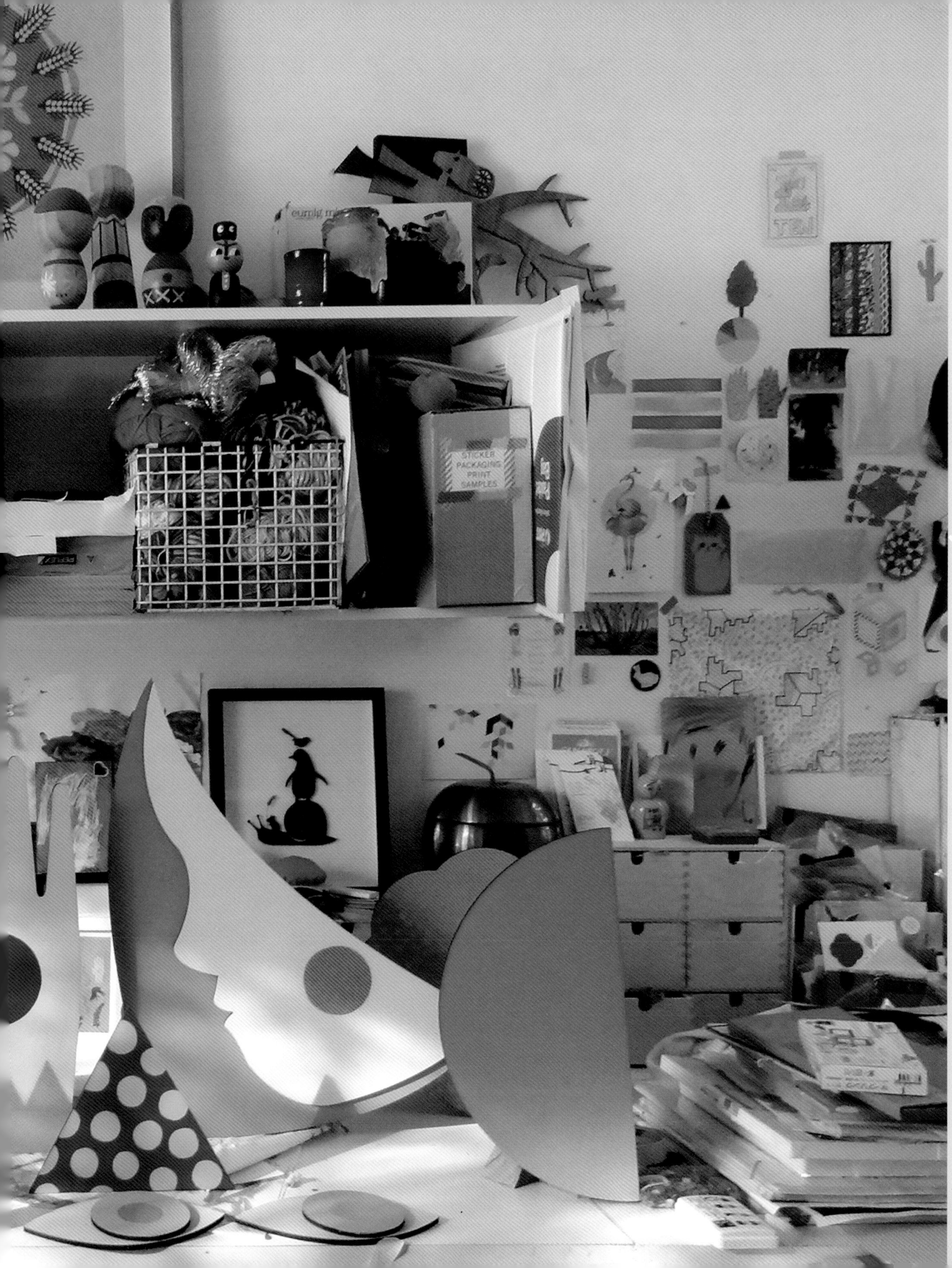
STICKER
PACKAGING
PRINT
SAMPLES

MAKE & DO

PAGE 143

WOOD
PROJECTS

WOOD LOVE

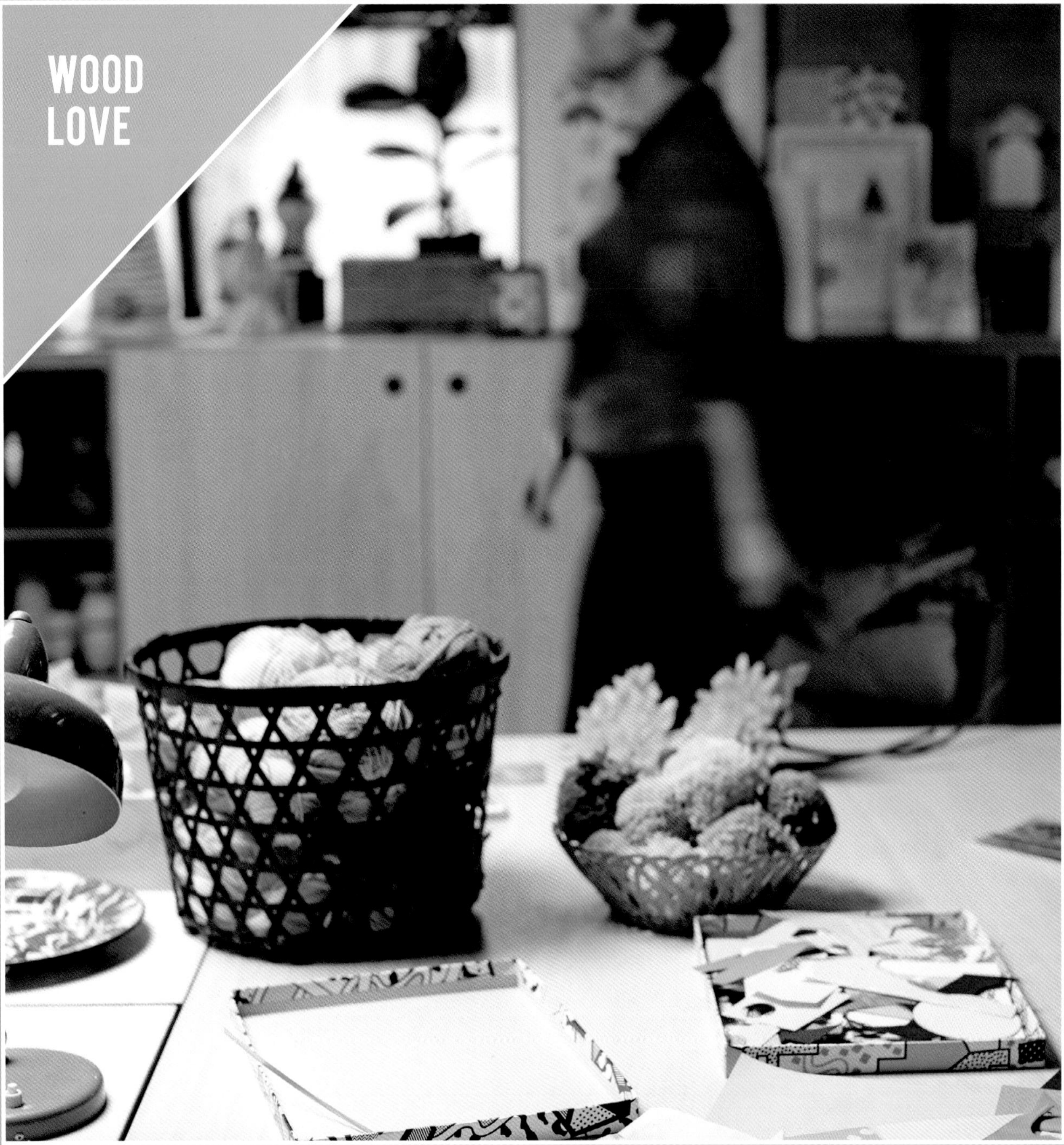

Unless you are quite comfortable working with wood and tools, the projects in this chapter are definitely the hardest. Wood can be scary to work with at first and mistakes can be expensive (and can hurt too), so the first rule is to take your time and plan out everything as much as possible. And don't be afraid to ask for help if you need it.

Making something from wood might be scary but it's equally rewarding. I've included some projects for beginners, which are good places to start if you are a bit nervous about the whole wood thing. Rest assured, once you get going you'll soon discover the awesome feeling one gets while working with power tools. Have faith – you can do it!

MAKE & DO

PAGE 150

GIANT WALL SPRINKLES

My partner, Raph, has a habit of becoming obsessed with perfecting a certain skill, which he then likes to turn into a business. One year it was burgers, and he started a burger truck. The next year it was tacos, and so we started a taco truck. This year it's donuts, and now we have a donut shop. Consequently, I've had donuts on the brain – and plenty in my mouth, too.

You'd think I'd be sick of donuts. I am a little tired of eating them, but I'm never bored of looking at them – they are my favourite 'graphic' food, so much so that they were the inspiration for this project. Surely everyone wants their lounge room to look like a giant donut? For extra donut-ty action, you could even paint the wall pink before adding the sprinkles – delicious!

This is a great project if you live in a rented property. The plywood strips are fairly light and can be attached by removable Velcro or adhesive strips.

DIFFICULTY (MEDIUM)

LET'S GO

1/

Using the ruler and pencil, mark up strips on the plywood measuring 21 cm (8¼ in) long and 5 cm (2 in) wide.

2/

Cut the strips lengthwise first, and then cut the lengths into the smaller strips.

3/

Use sandpaper to sand all the edges until smooth, then dust off with a cloth.

3/

4/

Paint the strips (I painted the front face only and not the sides).

TIP/ Depending on the type of paint and colour you are using, you may need a second coat. Make sure the first coat is dry before adding the second.

5 /

Use Velcro to attach the painted sprinkles to the wall, spacing them evenly apart and pointing them in random directions.

MAKE & DO

PAGE 155

FENCE POST BOOKENDS

You will need

* 2 decorative fence post tops (the ones I've used here are 'Windsor' and are available from larger hardware stores)
* handsaw
* medium-grit sandpaper
* cloth or rag
* sketchbook (see page 158)
* pencil
* paints
* paintbrushes
* masking tape
* clear matte varnish

If you don't feel confident about working with wood but still like the idea of making something with it, this project is for you. There's no hammer and nailing and only minimal sawing required.

This project is another born out of necessity – to keep my books in check in my new studio. I've wanted to do a bookend project for a while – one almost made it into my last book but I wasn't completely happy with it – and when I was wandering the aisles of my local hardware store, these rounded fence post tops jumped out at me. Looking at their shape, I could instantly picture them with faces and cute hats. The posts were quite heavy, so all I had to do was saw off the little end piece, paint in some details and *voilà* – bookends. The wood needs to be solid enough to hold up the books, so if your posts aren't very weighty, cut another piece of wood and fit it to the base.

DIFFICULTY
(EASY)

Give your little guys different facial expressions

Pretty up your shelf by adding washi tape

LET'S GO

1/

Saw the ends off both fence post tops.

2/

Use sandpaper to sand over the fence tops. Sand the bases to ensure your bookends will sit flat. Dust off with a cloth.

3/

Sketch out some design possibilities on paper. If your fence tops are a different shape, sketch out some ideas of how they could work as little guys.

3/

4/

Draw your design in pencil on the wood.

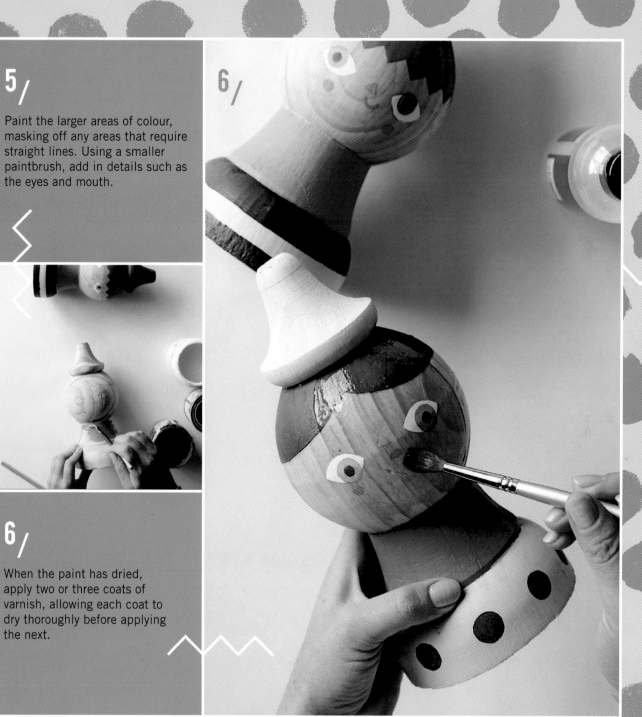

5/

Paint the larger areas of colour, masking off any areas that require straight lines. Using a smaller paintbrush, add in details such as the eyes and mouth.

6/

When the paint has dried, apply two or three coats of varnish, allowing each coat to dry thoroughly before applying the next.

6/

STORAGE BOXES

You will need

* approximately 83 x 120 cm (32¾ x 47¼ in) piece of 12 mm (½ in) plywood cut into:
  two (A) panels: 35 x 50 cm (13¾ x 19¾ in)
  two (B) panels: 32.6 x 35 cm (12¾ x 13¾ in)
  one (bottom) panel: 32.6 x 47.6 cm (12¾ x 18¾ in)
  four small squares for castors: 5 x 5 cm (2 x 2 in)
* ruler
* pencil
* jigsaw, handsaw or circular saw
* PVA glue
* approximately 40 x 1.25 mm (¹⁄₁₆ in) bullet head nails
* hammer
* coarse-grit sandpaper
* cloth or rag
* four 4 cm (1½ in) black rubber swivel castors
* 16 screws
* screwdriver
* masking tape
* acrylic paint
* paintbrushes

makes 1 storage box

Ahhhh, yes, the age-old storage question. If you are looking for something to put your things in that will look great and keep them neat and not cost a billion dollars and is not from Ikea like every other storage solution on the planet, then look no further. Making these storage boxes may not be as easy as assembling flat-pack shelves (which aren't that easy anyway), but it will be so much more satisfying knowing that you not only made this from scratch, but that you hand painted it as well.

I went to the extra trouble of adding castor wheels. At first I wasn't sure if that was overkill, but I've been using the boxes in my studio (they fit perfectly under my desk) and the castors are my favourite part – even more than the pink diagonal stripes!

NOTE / If you don't feel confident about cutting the wood, take the measurements and diagram on page 236 to your local hardware store, where they will be happy to cut the panels for you.

DIFFICULTY
(HARD)

These are so much
nicer than anything
store bought

LET'S GO

1/

Using the ruler and pencil, mark out the required lengths on the plywood.

2/

Cut out the panels.

3/

Mark the panels with 'A', 'B' and 'bottom', as indicated on page 236.

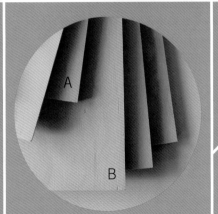

4/

Glue and then nail the A panels to the B panels, ensuring all the corners are flush.

TIP / Plywood has a 'wrong' side and a 'right' side, which is generally smoother.

4/

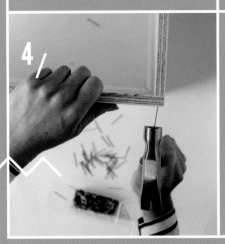

5/

Test the bottom piece to make sure that it fits. If it is a little too big, sand or lightly plane it to fit.

6 /

Glue and nail the bottom piece in.

7 /

When the glue is dry, sand over all the exterior panels. Dust off with a cloth.

6 /

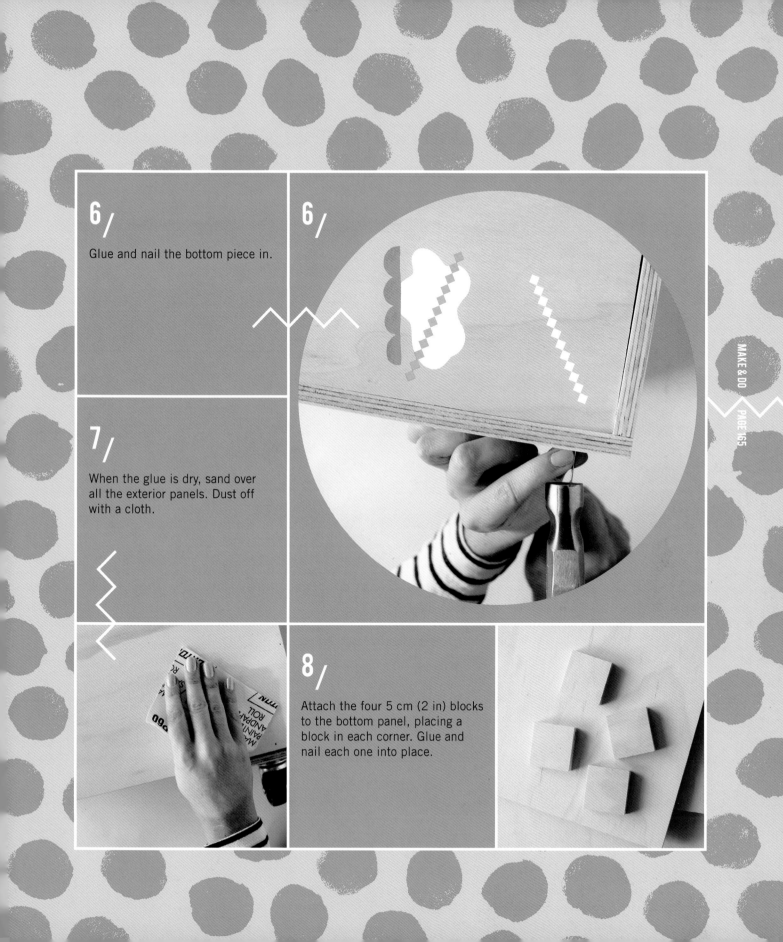

8 /

Attach the four 5 cm (2 in) blocks to the bottom panel, placing a block in each corner. Glue and nail each one into place.

9/

Screw in the four castors.

9/

10/

Consider your design, then pencil in or mask off the areas you want to paint.

11/

Paint your design. Apply two coats, allowing the first coat to dry before applying the second.

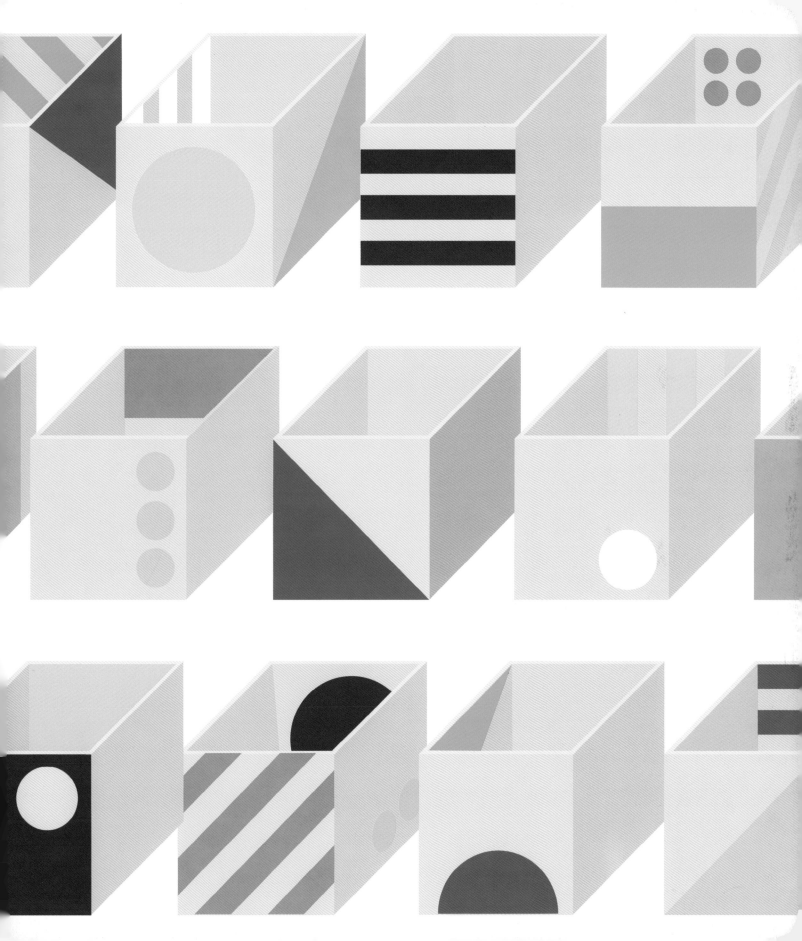

MONOCHROME RAINBOW SHELF

Sometimes I think my love for colour knows no bounds, but there are times when I do appreciate the simplicity of black and white. Of course, if it's going to be monochrome it still has to have lots of pattern – simplicity doesn't necessarily mean minimal! I love the way the monochrome paint tones on the rainbow work so well with the neutral tones of the plywood, which is why I have left some of the wood showing.

Part of the fun of this project is also planning what you're going to put on the shelf, in front of the rainbow. I think pastel or pale-coloured small objects work best, but the beauty of monochrome is that almost anything suits it.

DIFFICULTY
(MEDIUM)

How can you
be unhappy
if you have
a rainbow in
your room?

LET'S GO

1/

Rainbow
Measure and mark the centre point on one of the long edges of the plywood.

2/

Measure and then cut a 17.5 cm (7 in) length of string. Using one hand to hold the string on the centre point, and holding the pencil in your other hand, draw the radius on the wood. This line will form the inner edge of the rainbow.

TIP/ If you find it too hard to hold the string, secure one end of the string on the centre point with a piece of masking tape or a small thumbtack.

3/

Measure and then cut a 55 cm (21¾ in) length of string. Draw the outer edge of the rainbow.

TIP/ If you prefer a thinner rainbow, make the inner arch a little larger.

4 /

Carefully cut along the marked lines with the saw.

5 /

Use sandpaper to sand over the edges. Dust off with a cloth.

4 /

6 /

Following the photograph on page 169 as a guide, divide the rainbow into four sections. Draw the patterns onto each section of the rainbow. (Use the template for the long oval shapes or draw them freehand.)

7/

Mask off the diagonal pattern for the inner part of the rainbow. Paint all the areas of your design and leave to dry. Carefully remove the masking tape.

7/

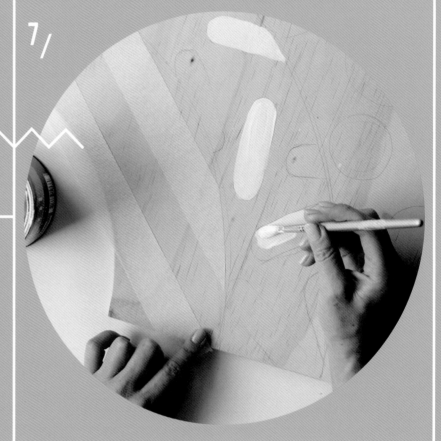

8/

Shelf
Following the manufacturer's instructions, install the wooden brackets onto the wall. Attach the pine shelf to the brackets (I used screws).

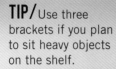

TIP/ Use three brackets if you plan to sit heavy objects on the shelf.

9/

Sit the rainbow on the shelf. To secure the rainbow in place, you can either screw or nail it to the top of the brackets (some wooden brackets extend a little bit above the shelf), or screw it to the wall. Alternatively, use a few strips of Velcro with adhesive backing.

DOLL'S HOUSE SHELF

You will need

* approximately 60 x 85 cm (23½ x 33½ in) piece of 12 mm (½ in) plywood cut into:

  two roof panels: 15 x 24.5 cm (6 x 9¾ in), with one side on each panel cut at a 45-degree mitre (the 15 cm/6 in side)

  two wall panels: 15 x 29.5 cm (6 x 11½ in), with one side on each panel cut at a 45-degree mitre (the 15 cm/6 in side)

  two panels for shelf and base: 15 x 27.5 cm (6 x 10¾ in)

  one back panel, with 2 small windows cut out (see Doll's House Shelf cutting guide, page 236)
* ruler
* pencil
* jigsaw or handsaw
* PVA adhesive
* hammer
* approximately 25 x 1.25 mm (¹⁄₁₆ in) bullet head nails
* coarse-grit sandpaper
* cloth or rag
* paper: white and coloured
* acrylic paints and paintbrushes
* masking tape
* scissors
* craft glue
* hooks, for hanging

If I had my way, I would still own a doll's house. Seriously, I often have to stop myself from buying miniature furniture on eBay. There is something about arranging tiny furniture in each tiny room that I find so irresistible. Throw a Sylvanian hedgehog family in there and I'm blissfully happy for hours! I have tried to enforce my love for dolls' houses on my own very boyish boys, but to no avail. So, instead, I decided to create this project – a doll's house masquerading as a shelf. Yes, it's a handy spot to store your favourite treasures, but the real beauty is that, when no one is looking, you can bring out that box of secretly purchased miniature furniture and lose yourself for hours.

My dad, Ross, made my first doll's house, and he also helped me make this one. Thanks again, Dad.

NOTE / This project requires some detailed cutting. If you don't feel confident, take the measurements and diagram on page 236 to your local hardware store and ask them to cut and mitre the wood for you.

DIFFICULTY
(HARD)

POTTERY AND PORCELAIN

51
WARNE

LET'S GO

1/

Using the ruler and pencil, mark out the required lengths on the plywood. Cut out the panels. Using a pencil, mark the panels for the roof and walls so they are easy to identify.

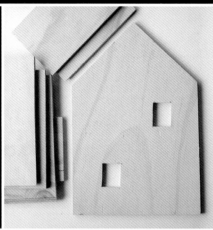

2/

Glue the two wall panels to the base panel, making sure the mitred ends of the wall panels are sitting at the top and facing out. Nail the panels in place.

3/

Glue and then nail the shelf in place.

3/

4/

Glue and nail the back piece.

5/

Glue and then nail the two roof panels together, making sure the mitred edges are neatly aligned.

6/

Glue the roof onto the back piece, then nail it into place. Sand all the surfaces, then dust off with a cloth.

5/

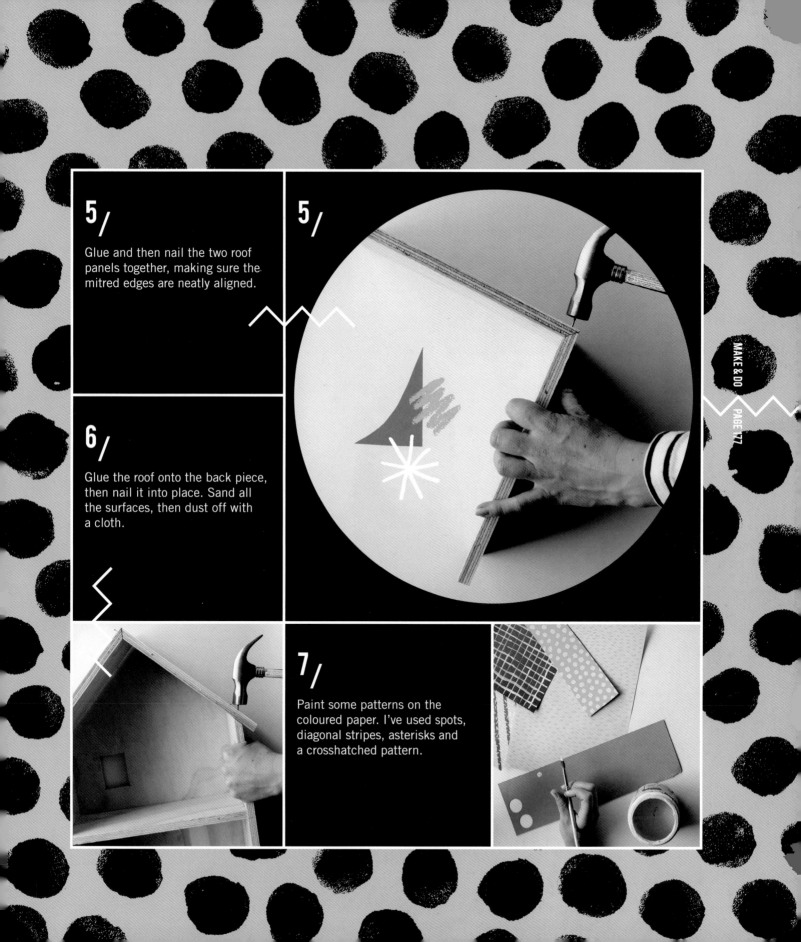

7/

Paint some patterns on the coloured paper. I've used spots, diagonal stripes, asterisks and a crosshatched pattern.

8 /

Mask off and paint some of the panels.

8 /

9 /

Cut the painted paper down to size and glue it in place.

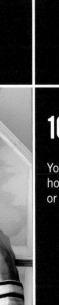

10 /

You can sit the finished doll's house shelf on an existing shelf or hang it on your wall.

FOUND

Using found things in a craft project is also about looking for materials in unusual places.

I've talked often about my collections – probably too much now – but recently I have (shockingly) found that I've wanted to clear out a bit of clutter. After years of collecting, I've started to feel my things are weighing me down and that I need a bit more creative breathing space. So, sadly, I've had to let some things go. Some bits and pieces have gone to the op shop, some to friends and some I have transformed into something new. This whole process has been quite cleansing and has also provided me with the inspiration for this chapter.

Using found things in a craft project is also about looking for materials in unusual places. If I have a certain project in mind, I try to keep that idea with me all the time, because often I find materials in the most unexpected places. For example, Asian grocery stores stock lots of brightly coloured plastic bits and pieces, fishing and tackle stores have beautiful rope, and even the plumbing section of the hardware store can provide some beautiful geometric pieces that can be used for making jewellery. I can't believe

I am owning up to this, but I have also been known to pick things up from the ground to use in projects (clean things, not gross things!). Just the other day I found the most amazing patterned paper in the gutter.

My occasional gutter picking is also part of my overall philosophy about re-using and recycling as much as possible. Finding an old treasure or reshaping something I already have into something new keeps me happy from an environmental point of view, too.

MAKE & DO
PAGE 186

卡ㄎㄚ車ㄔ truck

LEONARD COHEN AMSTERDAM, APRIL 1972

SORRY!

MAKE & DO
PAGE 193

FOUND PROJECTS

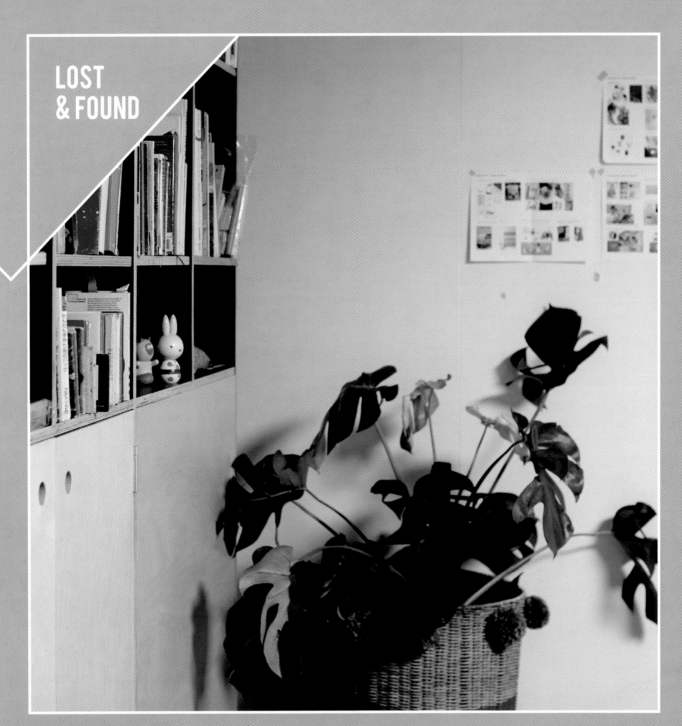

Taking an existing object or material, or something old and no longer of much use and then turning it into something new and beautiful can be quite a challenge, especially if this is a new process for you. It will draw upon all your creativity and imagination, but often the most challenging projects can be the most rewarding.

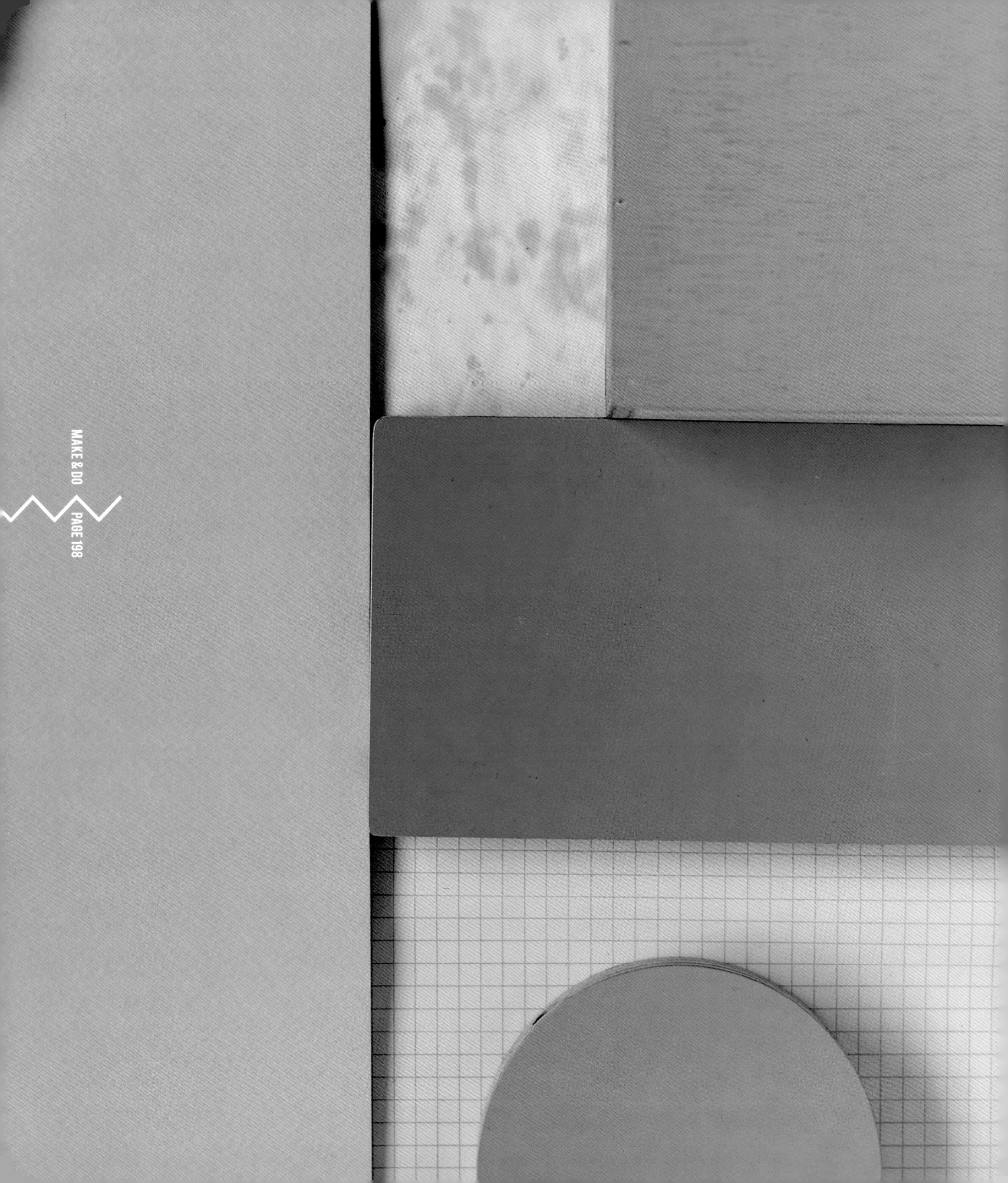

MAKE & DO
PAGE 198

FOUND & MADE NECKLACES

You will need

* different types of string or chain
* variety of beads: wooden, plastic, metal, recycled
* variety of other materials: plastic tubing, metal rings
* polymer clay
* kitchen knife
* toothpick or needle
* needle and cotton
* scissors
* necklace clasps

The thing about these necklaces is that, in all honesty, there isn't a lot to show you. It's more about the hunting and gathering process than the actual technique of how to make them.

I went to all the obvious places – craft stores, bead shops and the like – but I also went to non-necklacey type shops. In the plumbing section of the hardware store I found beautiful copper rings (albeit attached to other plumbing parts); in my local op shop I found some '80s necklaces, which I pulled apart for their plastic beads; and in my favourite stationery store I found some nice string. Online stores provide a plethora of amazing bead and other necklace discoveries, and don't forget about electrical supply stores and garden centres – these can be veritable treasure troves if you look with the right eyes.

You can also make parts of the necklace yourself. Polymer clay is lots of fun to play with, or you can revitalise plain wooden beads with some paint. I also braided some cotton to make a 'chain' for one of the necklaces.

DIFFICULTY
(MEDIUM)

LET'S GO

1/

Choose your favourite materials. Play around with the different elements to see what colours and textures work best together.

2/

Make some beads using polymer clay. You can use one colour or blend two colours together for a marbled look, add some small polka dots to a strip of clay, or twist two ropes of different colours together.

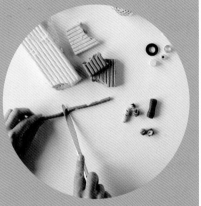

3/

For the polka dot beads, roll one colour of clay into your desired shape, then add some small 'dots' of a different coloured clay around the outside. Gently roll to combine (don't roll it too much).

4/

For the twisted rope beads, take two long, thin rolls of clay and twist them together. Cut to the desired length with a knife.

5/

Use a toothpick or needle to pierce a hole through the middle of all your clay beads. Following the manufacturer's instructions, bake the beads in the oven.

6/

To make a long curved bead, roll out the clay to the desired thickness and length, then push a toothpick through the middle to create a hole. Thread a needle with a piece of cotton and thread it through the hole.

5/

7/

Bend the bead to the desired shape. Remove the needle but leave the thread in the bead.

TIP / A toothpick gives a larger hole than a needle, making it easier to pass the thread through.

8 /

Bake the curved bead with the thread insitu (because polymer clay is usually baked at a low temperature, the thread won't burn). Remove from the oven and leave until cool enough to handle.

9 /

Select the string you'd like to use for your necklace and tie it to one end of the 'baked' thread. Pull the new string through the curved bead, then cut off and discard the baked thread.

9 /

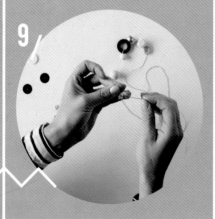

10 /

Thread all the beads onto the string or chain. If you like, add some knots along the string so that some of the beads sit higher than others.

11 /

When you are happy with the arrangement, work out the desired length and trim.

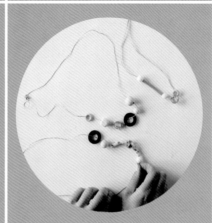

12 /

Tie on the clasps.

BUGHOUSES

You will need

* small cardboard box (with a removable lid)
* pencil
* craft knife or scalpel
* masking tape (use a low-tack tape if your cardboard isn't very thick)
* acrylic paint
* paintbrushes
* scissors
* flywire
* sticky tape or double-sided tape
* thin rope for handle

This project stems from a childhood love of collecting crawly things, which I then held captive in a bug-catcher – the plastic variety with a magnifying glass at the top. These cardboard bughouses don't have magnifying glasses, but they do have pretty spots and stripes, shaped flywire windows and a handle, too. If I were a captured bug, I know which one I'd prefer to live in.

I bought boxes from the craft store for this project, because I wanted some that were sturdy and had lids. You could use any small box, and if it doesn't have a lid, simply secure a piece of flywire over the top. You can buy rolls of flywire from the hardware store; make sure you choose a wire that is fine and flexible so it's easy to cut with scissors.

DIFFICULTY
(EASY)

LET'S GO

1/

Draw a doorway and some small windows on the box and lid. I've used a variety of shapes: circle, semicircle and rectangle.

2/

Carefully cut out the doorway and windows using a craft knife.

3/

Plan your design and use a pencil to draw on the stripes or spots. Mask off any areas that you want to paint.

3/

4/

Paint the stripes and spots, or your desired pattern, onto the box and lid. When the paint has dried, carefully peel off the masking tape.

5/

Cut the flywire to fit the windows and doorway.

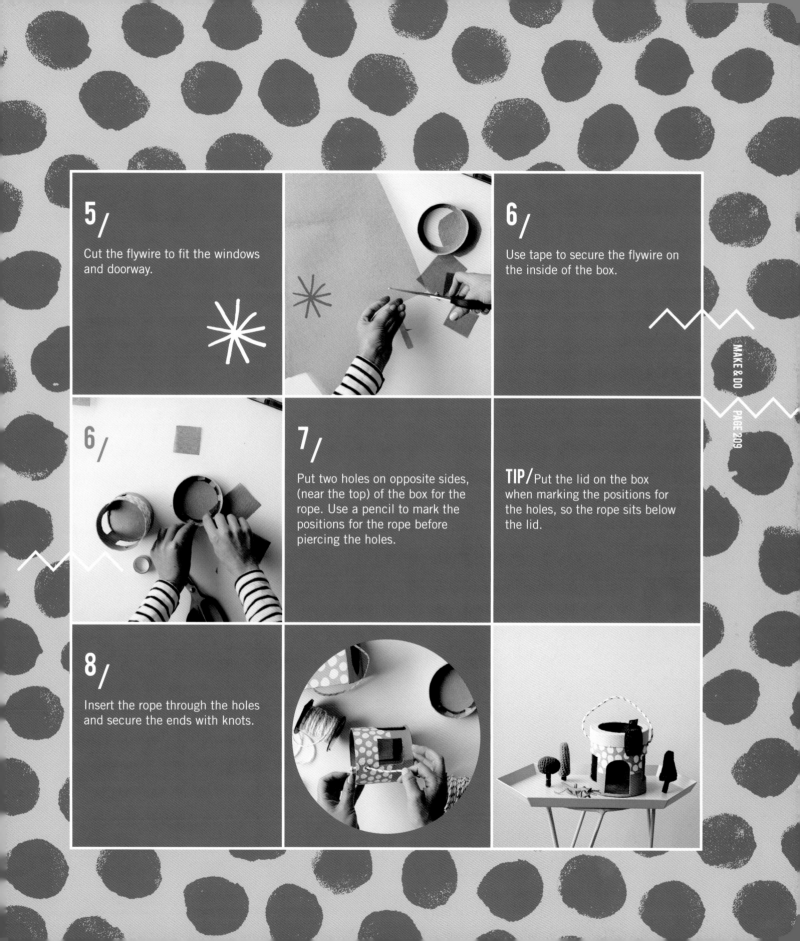

6/

Use tape to secure the flywire on the inside of the box.

6/

7/

Put two holes on opposite sides, (near the top) of the box for the rope. Use a pencil to mark the positions for the rope before piercing the holes.

TIP/ Put the lid on the box when marking the positions for the holes, so the rope sits below the lid.

8/

Insert the rope through the holes and secure the ends with knots.

WEAVING

You will need

* various items for weaving: haberdashery trims, paper, bias binding, ribbons, fabric scraps, nylon tape, mylar, netting

  I used 22 warp strips, 65–90 cm (25½–35½ in) in length and 24 weft strips, 60 cm (23½ in) in length. My strips were 2–2.5 cm (¾–1 in) wide.
* board or flat surface, to attach the weaving
* masking tape
* pins
* sewing machine or needle and thread
* handsaw
* balsa wood or stick, to attach at top
* cord or string
* drawing pins or thumbtacks
* double-sided tape or PVA glue

I'm absolutely loving the current resurgence of weaving. I've seen so many beautifully woven pieces lately that I felt quite inspired to make something similar, only to discover it required more tools (and possibly more skill) than I was prepared to use on this occasion. So I set about creating this little beauty instead. The method used is the most basic form of warp and weft weaving, using masking tape instead of a loom to secure the strips in place. I'm all for the occasional craft cheat here and there!

All the materials used in this weaving were either from the op shop or things that were already in my studio. You could use an infinite variety of materials for your weaving – as long as it's relatively flat and fairly flexible, then it's in.

I wanted this weaving to have a delicate and slightly transparent nature, so I kept my eye out for things with that look, and in keeping with its soft, floaty look, I varied the lengths of the warp strips, which I left hanging.

DIFFICULTY
(MEDIUM)

LET'S
GO

1/

Cut any extra-wide strips of fabric or trims to size.

2/

Lay out your 22 warp strips evenly along the top of the board and secure with masking tape.

3/

Starting from one side of the board, take a weft strip and weave it under and over the warp strips. Add a second weft strip, alternating the weave to achieve a chequerboard effect (see the diagram on page 214).

3/

4/

As you complete a row, secure the end with masking tape. Pin some areas in the weave to secure them.

TIP / Keep pushing the weft strips up so they are neat and tight.

5/

Once the weaving has reached the desired length, remove the masking tape off the board. Turn one side under and stick it to the back of the weaving with tape. Do the same for the other side and the top.

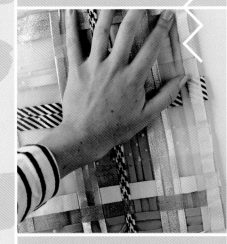

6/

If any areas in the centre of the weaving are looking loose, secure with small hand stitches.

6/

7/

Turn the masking-taped sides in once more to hide all the tape. Machine stitch or hand stitch the sides and top edge.

8/

Use the saw to cut the balsa wood to fit the width of the weaving.

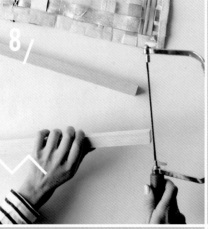

9/

Attach the cord to the balsa wood using small pins or thumbtacks.

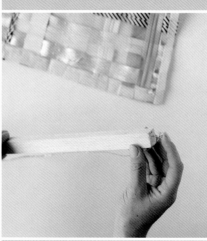

10/

Attach the weaving to the balsa wood using double-sided tape or PVA glue.

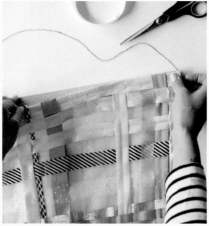

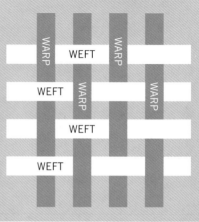

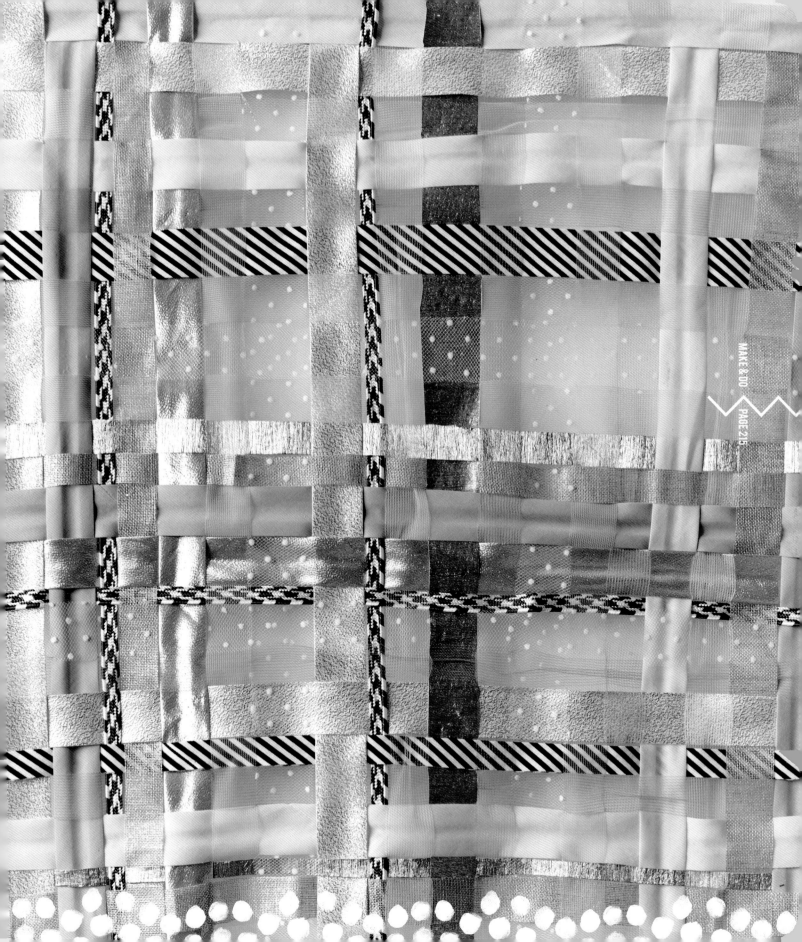

POMPOM
BASKETS

One of my theories in life is this: if you put a pompom on something, it instantly becomes better. This can be applied to many things, including cushions, headbands, cats and, now, wicker baskets.

Again, this is an easy project – but with maximum impact. The hardest part might be finding the baskets. I searched many places: the Swedish flat-pack furniture store once again came up trumps, and I also found some in our local discount store.

DIFFICULTY
(EASY)

Baskets make great containers for your plants

Fill baskets with your favourite cushions

LET'S GO

1/

Use a pencil to draw your design onto the basket.

TIP/A pencil is best for this; if you use a felt-tip pen in a dark colour, the outline may still be visible once the design is painted.

2/

If the design has straight edges, mask off the areas you don't want to paint.

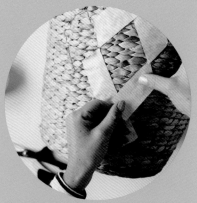

3/

Paint the design using acrylic paint. You will need two coats of paint to get an even coverage.

3/

4/

While the paint is drying, make your pompoms. Make sure you leave a long string on the end of each pompom for tying.

5/

Thread the long pompom string through the basket and tie a knot on the inside to fasten it.

6/

Work your way around the basket, securing the pompoms in place.

5/

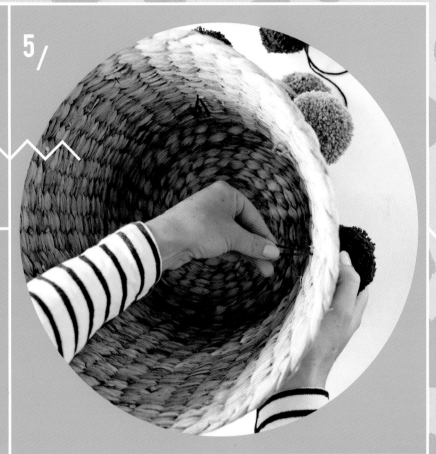

STYLE/

Tie a cute headscarf around your head and fill your basket with fruit. Pop it on your head and ta-da – Carmen Miranda!

PATTERNED ANIMAL GANG

You will need

* plastic animals (larger ones are easier to paint)
* spray paint
* acrylic paint
* scissors
* masking tape (look for one specifically designed to mask paint)
* paintbrushes
* small pompoms
* PVA glue
* pompom trim
* gold or silver glitter paper, for tiny crown

I've seen quite a few craft projects that use plastic animals. And no wonder; they are cheap, easy to find and it's not hard to take them from ordinary to a whole new level of totally awesome.

Take these guys, for example. All they needed was a bit of paint and some pattern and before long they started to develop their own personalities. There's Penelope Pony, the precious princess of the group; Taj Tiger, the reckless leader of the pack; and Gene Goat, quite clearly the joker … just to name a few. It's not hard to create your own animal gang – just let your imagination run wild.

DIFFICULTY
(EASY)

LET'S GO

1 /

Paint the plastic animals a base colour using either spray paint or acrylic paint.

2 /

To add a striped or diamond pattern, apply strips or small squares of masking tape over the animal and spray with a second colour. When the paint is dry, remove the tape.

3 /

To add squiggles, use a small paintbrush and acrylic paint to paint the pattern randomly over the animal.

4 /

To add pompoms, glue them in rows around the animal.

5 /

To add the dress-up detail, glue the pompom trim on.

6 /

Cut out and assemble a tiny crown. Glue the crown in place.

6 /

TIP /

Hold the trim in place with a pin while it dries.

JUMPER BLANKET

Is there anything cosier than a lap blanket on a cold night? Yes – a blanket made from jumpers! Throw in a stormy night, a cup of tea, an open fire and a warm cat at your feet and you may have just reached the pinnacle of cosiness.

I used nine jumpers for this project because I wanted to focus on using lots of different colours, so I ended up with quite a mix of fibres – wool, cotton, acrylic and even a bit of lamé (everything looks better with a touch of lamé). If you don't want to go for as many colours, you could get away with using four or five jumpers, depending on their size. If you choose all woollen jumpers, a good tip is to give them a hot wash beforehand, so they felt up and are easier to work with.

DIFFICULTY
(HARD)

LET'S GO

1/

Cut out the felt shapes from the templates.

TIP/ Felt templates are easier to use than paper because they 'stick' to the wool (or other fabric) and stay in place while cutting.

2/

Using the felt templates, cut out a variety of shapes from all the jumpers.

TIP/ Use the pockets and ribs from a few jumpers, to add texture and interest.

3/

Arrange your fabric shapes in an order or pattern large enough to form a blanket. You may need to go back and cut out a few extra pieces to fill any holes.

3/

4/

Using small pieces of masking tape and a pen, number and label all your fabric pieces in order.

TIP/ Take a photo of the arrangement on your phone, to use as a visual reference.

5/

Pin the shapes together.

6/

Tack the pieces together with running stitch, allowing a 1 cm (½ in) seam allowance.

5/

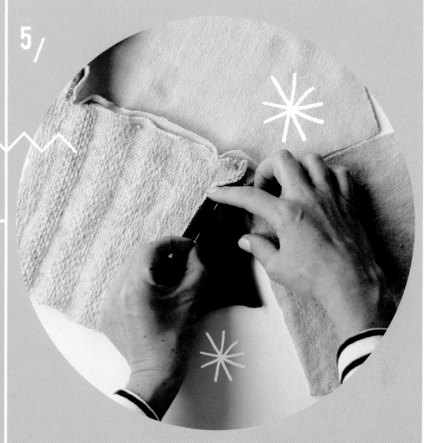

7/

Sew all the pieces together with a sewing machine (you may need to adjust the tension on your machine if you are using different fabrics). Cut off the excess pieces to form straight edges. Give the final square a press with an iron.

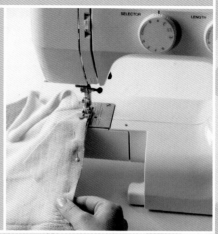

8 /

Cut the backing fabric to size. Pin it together with the right sides of the blanket and backing facing in. Sew the pieces together, leaving a 20 cm (8 in) gap unsewn.

9 /

Turn the blanket right side out through the gap. Close the hole with hand stitching.

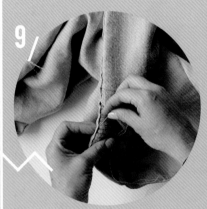

9 /

10 /

10 /

Insert pins into the middle of each patch to mark where you want to add a cross-stitch. Add small gold cross-stitches to secure the front to the backing.

TEMPLATES

BATIK FUROSHIKI

BASIC WRAP

FOUR-TIE WRAP

MY FAVOURITE LYRICS

INCREASE TO 200% ON PHOTOCOPIER

Cut 1

Cut 1

Cut 1

TONIGHT I'M SWIMMING TO MY FAVOURITE ISLAND

Cut 2

Cut 1

Cut 1

Cut 1

Cut 1

Cut 10

Cut 3   Cut 4

Cut 1

Cut 1

PAPER BROOCHES

SHAPES ARE 100%, cut 2 each
(and 1 only for the cylinder brooch)

JUMPER BLANKET

INCREASE TO 250% ON PHOTOCOPIER

B

D

C

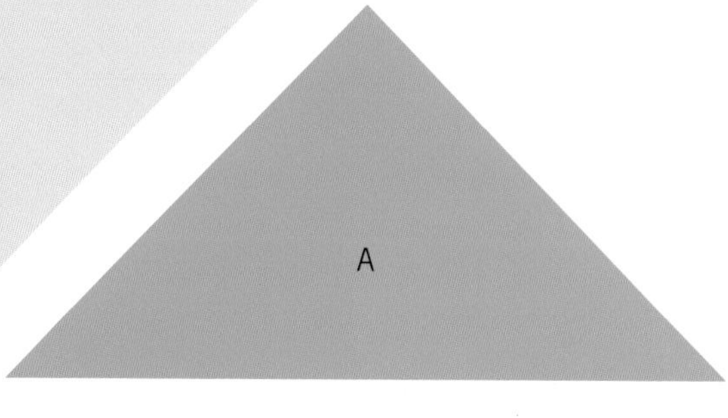

A

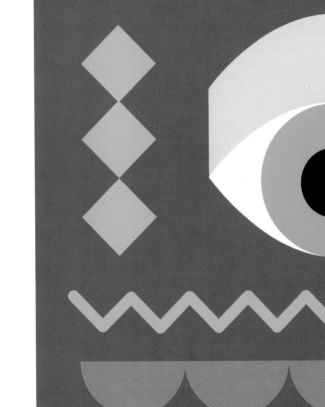

SURPRISE BALL
SEAL, 100%, cut 2

SHIRTLESS COLLAR
EMBROIDERY, 100%

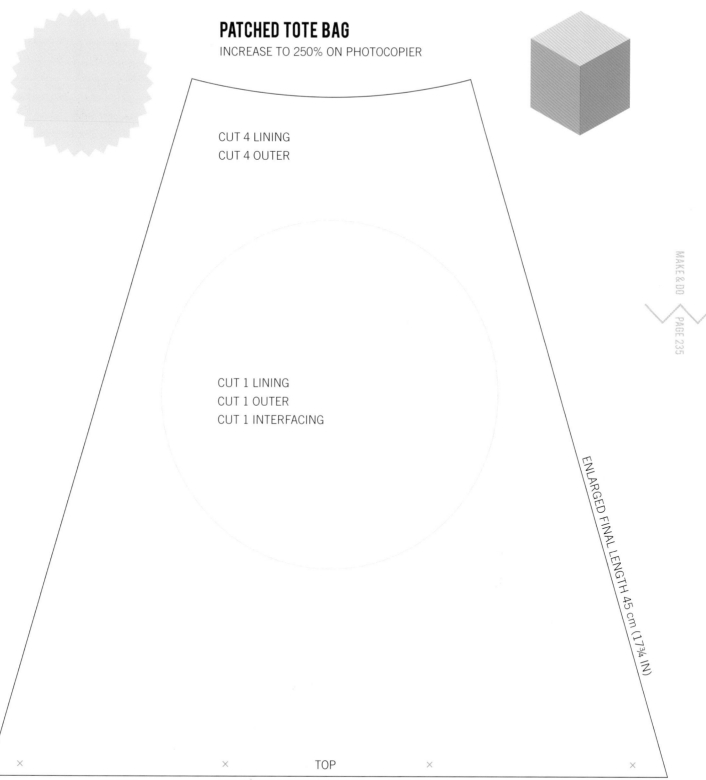

PATCHED TOTE BAG
INCREASE TO 250% ON PHOTOCOPIER

CUT 4 LINING
CUT 4 OUTER

CUT 1 LINING
CUT 1 OUTER
CUT 1 INTERFACING

ENLARGED FINAL LENGTH 45 cm (17¾ IN)

TOP

RIVETS   ENLARGED FINAL WIDTH 35 cm (13¾ IN)

MAKE & DO
PAGE 235

DOLL'S HOUSE SHELF
CUTTING GUIDE (NOT TO SCALE)

RAINBOW SHELF
LONG OVAL SHAPE, 100%

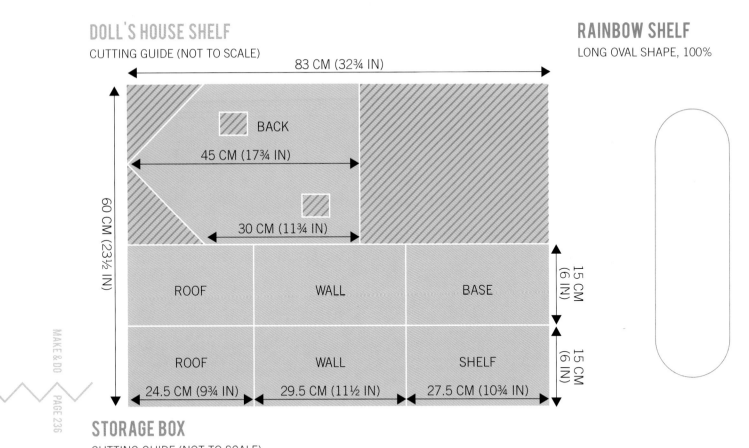

83 CM (32¾ IN)

BACK

45 CM (17¾ IN)

30 CM (11¾ IN)

60 CM (23½ IN)

ROOF

WALL

BASE

15 CM (6 IN)

ROOF

WALL

SHELF

15 CM (6 IN)

24.5 CM (9¾ IN)

29.5 CM (11½ IN)

27.5 CM (10¾ IN)

STORAGE BOX
CUTTING GUIDE (NOT TO SCALE)

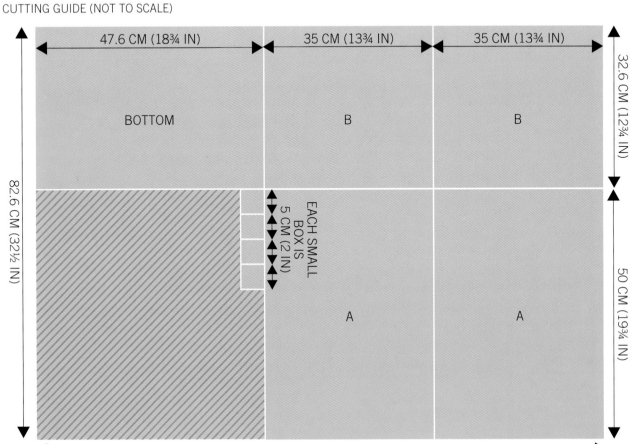

47.6 CM (18¾ IN)

35 CM (13¾ IN)

35 CM (13¾ IN)

32.6 CM (12¾ IN)

BOTTOM

B

B

EACH SMALL BOX IS 5 CM (2 IN)

82.6 CM (32½ IN)

A

A

50 CM (19¾ IN)

118 CM (46½ IN)

PAPIER MÂCHÉ
PAINTING GUIDE

BASE PIECES
INCREASE TO 200% ON PHOTOCOPIER

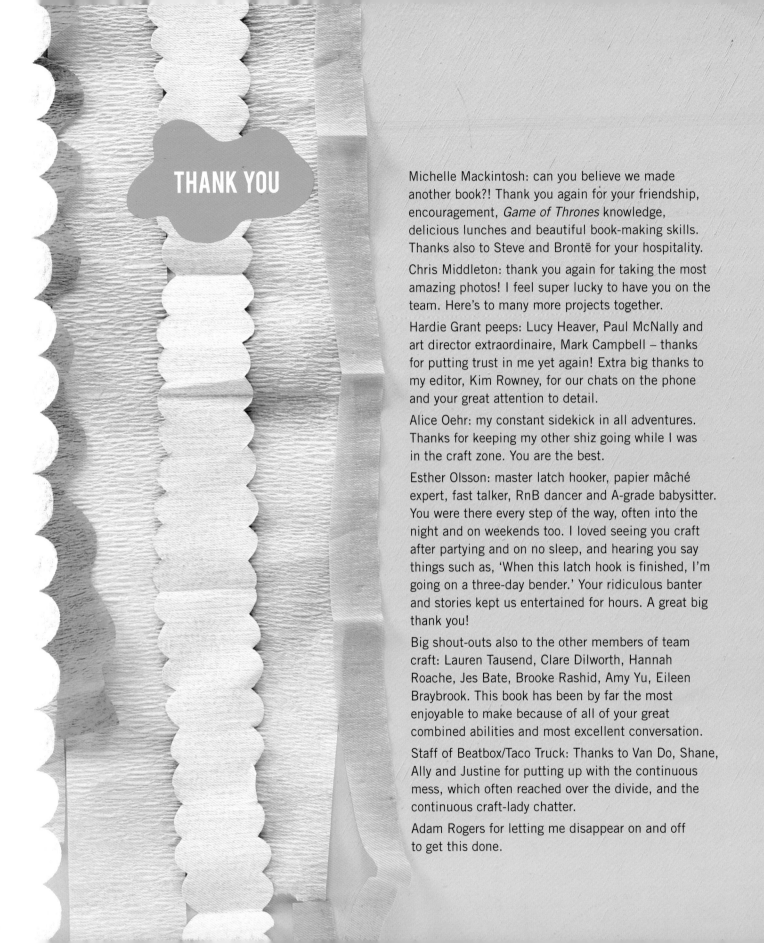

THANK YOU

Michelle Mackintosh: can you believe we made another book?! Thank you again for your friendship, encouragement, *Game of Thrones* knowledge, delicious lunches and beautiful book-making skills. Thanks also to Steve and Brontë for your hospitality.

Chris Middleton: thank you again for taking the most amazing photos! I feel super lucky to have you on the team. Here's to many more projects together.

Hardie Grant peeps: Lucy Heaver, Paul McNally and art director extraordinaire, Mark Campbell – thanks for putting trust in me yet again! Extra big thanks to my editor, Kim Rowney, for our chats on the phone and your great attention to detail.

Alice Oehr: my constant sidekick in all adventures. Thanks for keeping my other shiz going while I was in the craft zone. You are the best.

Esther Olsson: master latch hooker, papier mâché expert, fast talker, RnB dancer and A-grade babysitter. You were there every step of the way, often into the night and on weekends too. I loved seeing you craft after partying and on no sleep, and hearing you say things such as, 'When this latch hook is finished, I'm going on a three-day bender.' Your ridiculous banter and stories kept us entertained for hours. A great big thank you!

Big shout-outs also to the other members of team craft: Lauren Tausend, Clare Dilworth, Hannah Roache, Jes Bate, Brooke Rashid, Amy Yu, Eileen Braybrook. This book has been by far the most enjoyable to make because of all of your great combined abilities and most excellent conversation.

Staff of Beatbox/Taco Truck: Thanks to Van Do, Shane, Ally and Justine for putting up with the continuous mess, which often reached over the divide, and the continuous craft-lady chatter.

Adam Rogers for letting me disappear on and off to get this done.

James Reynold for the woodworking advice and help.

Ross Orpin for helping to transform our warehouse into a temporary photography studio.

Max Olijnyk for lending me your cameras.

Nat Turnbull for styling help. Next time I need you full time, please.

Ricky Do for helping with all the background painting and running around.

For generously lending me your lovely wares (some for the third year in a row): Mr Kitly, Scout House, Loom Rugs, After, Pan After, P.A.M, Angelucci 20th Century, Third Drawer Down, The Junk Company, Arro Home, Takeawei, Monk House, Kuwaii and Stephanie Somebody. Please support these amazing stores/labels/people.

Kirra Jamison, Alice Oehr, Michelle Mackintosh and Natalie Turnbull also kindly provided additional props from their personal treasure troves.

Tyke, Ari and Raph: as always you are the people who really keep me going. All my entire love and everything for you guys. Tio and Miso, you guys are also great.

My amazing mum: you go out of your way to help us live this crazy life we got ourselves into. Thanks for your continuous support and for forgiving me a thousand times over when I am snappy and grumpy.

The rest of my beautiful family: Dad, Erwin, Emily, Sean, Sam and Joe, Leslie, Rudin, Brooke, Zedrin, Joh, Andie, Annie and Norm and the extended D'Arcy and Orpin clan.

The super nice Melbourne folk who let me in to photograph their studios: Emily Green, Kit Palaskas, Peaches + Keen, Miso, Magda Ksiezak (okay Kiosk), Cathy Tippy, Tin & Ed, Lara and Jess from Homework, Lucas Grogan, Sandra Eterovic, Penelope Durston, Alice Oehr, Minna Gilligan, Kirra Jamison and Dear Plastic.

Nice people who help and support me: Jeremy Worstman and Jacky Winter, Lucy and Lisa from The Design Files, Jason Grant, Megan Morton, *Inside Out* magazine, The Thousands, Koskela, Craft Victoria, *Frankie* magazine, Rae Ganim, the Rogers family, Karen Batson, Camillo and Monica Ippoliti, plus all my lovely LOVELY freelance clients.

Shauna T: My friend who understands it all. Thank you x 1,000,000.

My other beautiful friends: Chris Midds; Kirra; Amanda, Conor, Bonnie and Corey; Rosie, Max and Tess; Misha and Odi; Olivia, Ed, Fia and Milo; Nat and Frank; Lawrence; Daniel and Emma; Elska, Marcus and Izzi; Kellie, Cameron and Ralph; Tai and family; Malcolm and Maurice; Tristan, Age and Teenie; Sue, Marta and Claude; Adeline and Rohan; Dee, Andrew and Harry; and everyone else too (you know who you are!).

Music was an important part of making this book and I would like to express my gratitude to community radio (specifically Melbourne stations RRR and PBS) for supporting indie music and always giving me something great to listen to.

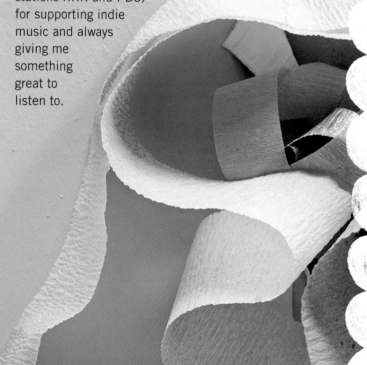

Published in 2014 by Hardie Grant Books

Hardie Grant Books (Australia)
Ground Floor, Building 1
658 Church Street
Richmond, Victoria 3121
www.hardiegrant.com.au

Hardie Grant Books (UK)
5th & 6th Floor
52–54 Southwark Street
London SE1 1RU
www.hardiegrant.co.uk

A Cataloguing-in-Publication entry is available
from the catalogue of the National Library of
Australia at www.nla.gov.au

Make & Do
ISBN: 978 1 74270 841 6

Publishing Director: Paul McNally
Managing Editor: Lucy Heaver
Editor: Kim Rowney
Design Manager: Mark Campbell
Designer: Michelle Mackintosh
Photographer: Chris Middleton
Production Manager: Todd Rechner
Production Coordinator: Carly Milroy
Colour reproduction by Splitting Image
Colour Studio
Printed in China by 1010 Printing International
Limited

Hardie Grant and Beci Orpin would like
to thank Koskela and Ashley Jones for
the use of images in this book.